Solfege Teaching Guide

First Edition

Eileen Sauer

Solfege Teaching Guide

First Edition
Version 1.1
Last updated: 2/15/2021

Copyright © 2018 by Eileen Sauer
ISBN: 1-979-64193-5

Cover illustration by Daniel Fidoten

Contents

Background ... 6
Preparatory Work ... 12
    Dannhäuser Solfege ... 13
    Accompaniment Book ... 15
    Dictation Book ... 16
    Whiteboard / Chalkboard ... 17
    Seating ... 18
    Two Pianos ... 20
    Supplies ... 22
Structure of Classes ... 24
    Student Growth (long term) ... 28
    Teacher Growth (long term) ... 30
    Solfege Process Growth ... 31
Running a Demonstration ... 32
Launching a New Class ... 35
    First Solfege Class ... 36
    First Dictation Class ... 43
    Joining an Existing Class ... 46
    Teenage / Adult Students ... 47
    Taking A Step Back ... 48
    Administrative Considerations ... 50
    New Solfege Instructors ... 51
Mozart Effect DIY Kit ... 54
Foundation - Details ... 58
    Sight Singing ... 59
    Sightreading ... 61
    Conducting Time ... 65

- Ear Training ... 68
- Music Dictation ... 78
- Improving Solfege Skills ... 82
  - Continuity Rule ... 83
  - Got It, Forgot It ... 86
  - Tackle the Hardest First ... 87
  - Mental Play ... 88
- Adding to the Foundation ... 91
  - Church Modes ... 92
  - Meter Lesson ... 94
  - Beaming Notes ... 98
  - Lead Sheets ... 99
  - ABRSM ... 101
- Using Solfege as a Tool ... 102
  - Improvisation ... 104
  - Composition ... 107
- Music Notation Software ... 115
  - Sibelius Notation Checklist ... 117
- Advanced Students ... 127
  - Coaching Leaders ... 128
  - Advanced Exercises ... 132
- Performance Preparation ... 133
  - History ... 134
  - Tips and Tricks ... 140
- Curriculum ... 148
  - Level 1 ... 150
  - Level 2 ... 152
  - Level 3 ... 154
  - Level 4 ... 155
  - Level 5 ... 156
- Exercises ... 157

Sample 1	158
Sample 2	159
Sample 3	161
Sample 4	164
Archives	166
Synesthesia	172
Piano Practice	178
New Students	179
Le Carpentier	183
References	194
Acknowledgements	196
About the Author	198

Background

Mademoiselle Yvonne Combe studied music at the Paris Conservatory when French composers Claude Debussy, Gabriel Fauré, Camille Saint-Saëns and Maurice Ravel were alive and Fauré was Director of the Conservatory. She taught in Paris, France and Montreux, Switzerland, then later emigrated to the US and founded The French School of Music in Plainfield, NJ in 1927, teaching piano and solfege in the U.S. for over six decades. I took piano and solfege lessons at French School from 1972 to 1982 (ages 7 - 17), when Mlle. Combe was in her 80s. Many French School alumni competed in NJ MEC (Music Education Council) piano competitions, and as first, second, or third place winners, performed in Carnegie Recital Hall. I played there nine times, and my little sister played there ten times. There are Carnegie programs with 12 French School students listed. Back then I thought all of this was "normal" and couldn't understand why students of other piano teachers weren't doing the same thing, because it all seemed relatively easy.

Of the French School alumni in the 1970s (and a few before and after), these are the known alumni who went to Juilliard or pre-Juilliard:

- Jim Correnti (also Reformed Episcopal Seminary)
- Julie Jacobson (also Fordham University, NY Restaurant School)
- Robert Taub (also Princeton) (check Wikipedia)
- Karen Zereconsky (also Manhattan School of Music and Moscow Conservatory of Music)

- Mayo Tsuzuki (also Yale)
- Wendy Jaffe (also Duke University)
- Eri Ikezi (also Columbia University)

Other alumni include:

- Carol Comune (New England Conservatory)
- Vince Di Mura (Manhattan School of Music)
- Liz Du Four (University of Ottawa)
- Timothy Waters (Principia College), specializing in acoustic, audiovisual, and technology design for performance venues (requiring knowledge of music and physics)
- Suzanne Waters (Principia College), professional singer who has worked in many films and television series (check IMDB), also a graphic and web designer

Alumni from these lists who are past and present faculty include Vince Di Mura and Carol Comune at Princeton, and Karen Zereconsky at Princeton, French Conservatory, and conservatories in Asia and Italy. Alumni have been / are resident artists and composers as well as concertizing artists. Mayo Tsuzuki worked with Zubin Mehta, and Vince Di Mura studied with Constance Keene.

Those alumni who did not pursue careers as professional musicians became doctors, lawyers, technologists, entrepreneurs, executives, etc. I became a software developer, technical trainer and engineering manager (University of Notre Dame), real estate investor, and also a self-taught composer who as of spring 2016 became the eighth known alumna to have joined the Juilliard ranks, part of the evening division taking classes in music composition and orchestration.

Alumni from earlier decades who reconnected with the school through the French School of Music Facebook page also show a pattern of successful musical careers as performers, music educators, etc. Because of Mlle. Combe's history with the Paris Conservatory and her methodologies, French School students often developed both excellent technique and a musical voice informed by French composers.

After a lifetime dedicated to teaching piano and solfege, Mlle. Combe passed away in 1990 at age 97. Her student Stephen Waters took over the school, and in 2014 he passed away as well, putting the school's fate at a crossroad. Judy Waters took over as director of the school, and in late 2015, she asked me to restart solfege classes at French School, which hadn't been offered in a few years. By then, the days of Mlle. Combe requiring piano students to take solfege lessons had ended. There can be various obstacles to taking and teaching solfege classes. Parents may not want to make multiple trips to the school every week, and students today are involved in more and more activities that leave insufficient time for learning solfege. Piano teachers may be so busy with piano students that they don't have time to run solfege classes.

At French School, what was lost in terms of extra time and effort needed for solfege classes, was repaid when it took months, not years, to learn to perform increasingly advanced music because instrument and voice lessons became that much more efficient.

When Judy asked me to restart solfege classes, I had never stepped into a conservatory environment, and her request prompted me to simultaneously enroll in Juilliard. Three months after we restarted solfege classes, one student surprised her parents by performing a solo at a school event. At the one year mark, two students had begun to develop absolute pitch (meaning without the aid of a pitch pipe, they could identify the pitch of a note, the same way those who are not color blind can identify a blue sweater). At the two year mark, a 5th grader played recorder, ukelele, jazz saxophone, and some piano. When asked what music training they get in their schools, the universal response is crinkled faces and "that stuff is so *easy*!!".

The French School methodology uses a *fixed do* system where syllables are always tied to specific pitches, as opposed to *movable do*. This is an approachable yet powerful four prong methodology for gaining a deep understanding of music through singing / sightreading on pitch while solfegiating the notes, conducting time, ear training, and music dictation. Solfege can also be used as a tool for studying improvisation and music composition.

The combination of piano lessons and solfege classes made success possible for so many French School alumni. Those who take piano and solfege lessons run through a thought process when a teacher presents a new piece during a piano lesson. That process may look something like this:

Focus on the right hand: treble clef, two sharps in the key signature: fa and do. Take the last sharp which is do, go up one note, re, so the song is in re major. Many French School alumni can sing on pitch and figure out the timing, and will sing the music in their head. Maybe it sounds like a joyous Irish dance.

They would place the right hand on the keyboard and...

That doesn't sound too good. The piano teacher would then help students develop whatever technique is needed to handle the more challenging passages.

The joyous Irish dance students hear in their heads might not sound quite right when they play it. And the piano teacher would help students develop the muscle memory to fully express the musicality.

This is what a piano lesson *should* be like. Solfege teaches foundational elements of music so that students can spend their piano lesson time focusing on technique and musical expression.

Not all alumni developed absolute pitch, but given a starting note, most could mentally solfege a new piece they wanted to learn. What occurs mentally for solfege students is the same thing that occurs in a piano teacher's head. Everyone is on the same page when the fundamentals are nailed down, and students and teachers can focus on refinement.

In the French School archives, one recital program mentions a 2 ½ year old student giving a recital. The French School solfege method is accessible even to the very young, and students begin creating music from day one.

While there are multiple ways to skin a cat, this guide will explain the French School solfege methodology, as well as fill in relevant gaps encountered in a conservatory environment. In addition, students taking piano lessons may want to look at my dad's book *Fundamentals of Piano Practice* (see References at the end), which explains Mlle. Combe's methodology for efficient piano practice. The piano practice and solfege teaching guides provide a comprehensive treatment of her entire methodology. The online training bootcamps covering the solfege exercises put this methodology into practice.

In closing, here is an email from Grace Nocera Boeringer (one of French School's earliest students, now in her 80s in 2018 and still a performing violinist).

> Dear Eileen, Judy, Wayne and all the others,
>
> Thank you all for reviving this marvelous tradition (Solfege) that I grew up with many years ago. I am so thankful for the training I had and want you all to know how much pleasure and ease it gave me in my career in music.
>
> I remember well those classes with Mlle. Combe, Mlle. Pfeiffer and Madame Seguin. Not only were they musically very instructive, they were FUN!! We formed a great "support" group. I will always remember those days.
>
> Very Best Wishes,
>
> Grace Nocera Boeringer

If, like Grace, you would like to find a "pleasure and ease" that will lead to a lifelong love of music, then let us get started.

Eileen Chang Sauer (French School '72 - '82)

Preparatory Work

Start by assembling the proper classroom setup and supplies:

- Dannhäuser solfege book 1 and piano accompaniment book

- Dictation books / pencils / lapboards

- Folding chairs

- White board / black chalkboard with lines

- Markers / chalk

- Music stands around the piano

- Music flash cards to test pitches, note durations, sharps and flats, etc.)

Dannhäuser Solfège des Solfèges

Book I contains 171 short exercises that students can sightread. They begin by introducing whole notes, then half notes, intervals, whole rests, and progressing one step at a time. Toward the end, Book I introduces bass clef and different key signatures other than do major scale. Advanced French School students use to progress to a blue book titled Solfege d'Artiste but this is no longer in print, therefore no longer covered. The Dannhäuser exercises are fun to sightread and sing, and are not childish, boring, or non-musical.

Book II contains 90 exercises that are longer and more advanced, with more advanced key signatures and covering ornaments like appoggiatura, cadenza, etc.

Book III contains 66 exercises that are more advanced, and also cover alto and tenor clef.

There are two online Make Music Now! bootcamps that cover Books I and II. We do not cover Book III.

Accompaniment Book

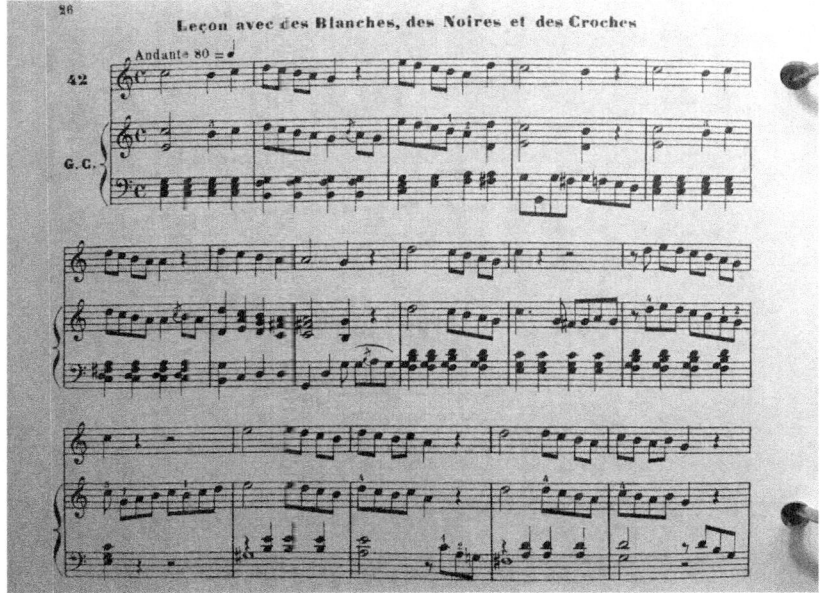

The piano accompaniment book contains both the vocal melody as well as piano accompaniment. For some reason, these books are no longer available online or for sale, but we have the original accompaniment books for Book I and II. We do not have the piano accompaniment for Book III. However, I came up with an accompaniment for Exercise 1 in Book III, in the style of what the French composers did for Books I and II. This would be an ambitious project for a later time if there is demand.

Dictation Book

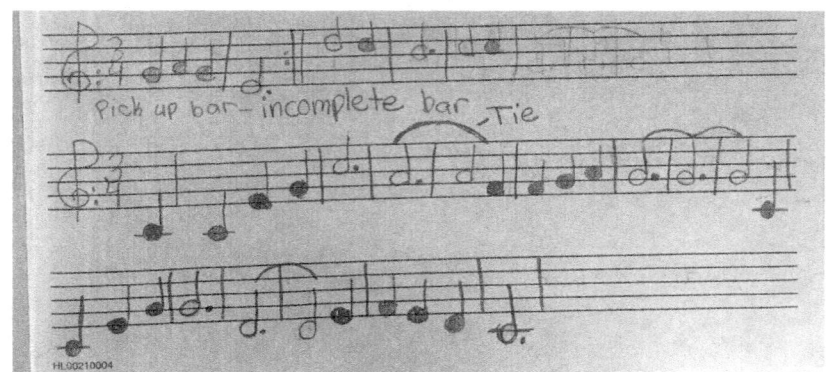

Each student will have a blank music notebook for doing dictation. Dictation is done once a month during the last solfege class of each month.

Whiteboard / Chalkboard

This is a whiteboard with music staff on it, and magnetic buttons to use as notes. Another useful tool is a black chalkboard with white lines painted on it.

Seating

Have folding chairs in a range of heights, with shorter chairs in front and higher chairs in back. Students find a seat that is the appropriate height for them, so that when they are singing solfege or doing dictation, their solfege or dictation book sits horizontally and stable on their laps when their feet are flat on the ground.

Place folding chairs on the right far enough away from walls or cabinets so that students don't hit the wall or cabinet when conducting time. Place chairs far enough apart for students to conduct time without hitting each other.

There are benches and chairs in the back of the class for parents who want to stay during class. For very young students, the advantage is that parents serve as surrogates outside of the school so that their children won't practice something incorrectly for an entire week.

Two Pianos

French School has two pianos in one room for ear training. The instructor plays something on the first piano and the student replicates what is played on the second piano.

This allows everyone - students, teachers, and parents - to immediately assess who is good at ear training, and who is hunting and pecking trying to find the right key. This system works well, whether or not listeners have absolute pitch.

More importantly, students will slowly graduate from doing single note ear training, to identifying two note chords, then three note chords, and so on. Without two keyboards in one room, students would not be able to hear multiple notes played simultaneously, then play them back on the second keyboard. If it's not feasible to have two pianos in one room, at least have two inexpensive keyboards, one in front of the other so that the student can sit in front of the teacher. Whenever I go to a music school or conservatory, I consider two keyboards in one room to be a litmus test for whether or not institutions are able to do ear training the way we did at French School. In my experience, when I test even people with music degrees, who haven't had two piano ear training, even some of the more basic French School ear training tests will throw them off.

The following addition to the above process makes ear training even more effective. Start with the do major scale, and specify a base note and a simple interval. If the student is advanced and has absolute pitch or is close to having absolute pitch, have them sing the base note and correct second note for the interval, then play the notes on the piano. If they are not as advanced, the instructor can optionally play the base note on the piano for reference. For example:

Instructor: do sixth

Student: sings do la, then plays do and la on the keyboard

Advantages to this addition:

- Students who want more ear training or are serious about developing absolute pitch can practice on their own.

- Unlike straight two piano ear training, students must actively engage in mental play to hear the notes in their head before they can sing them.

Students may be inaccurate for several reasons:

- Their mental play for the notes is incorrect, because they don't have absolute pitch or absolute relative pitch yet.

- Their mental play for the notes is correct, however, the vocal musculature is untrained enough, or they are not warmed up enough yet, that physically the wrong note comes out. If this is the case, students can indicate this and try again. This is also why starting with a note in a comfortable vocal range (like middle do) is advantageous. This is much harder if the starting base note is very high or very low.

Supplies

Place 3 - 5 music stands around the piano for each group of students to sight sing while conducting time. Ensure younger students use music stands closest to the accompanist so that the accompanist can monitor if they are beating time correctly, and emphasize the first beat if necessary.

Use markers for the white board, chalk for blackboard, pencils for dictation, and lapboards where students can place their dictation books on their laps and write (since we use stools instead of desks).

Have extra solfege books in case someone forgets or loses theirs; students can also share with other students. Since dictation is only once a month, students leave their dictation books at the school so they don't get lost.

Have an award cabinet with prizes on display. Solfege students get 3 points if they make a clear effort to improve. They can get 1 bonus point if they do something perfectly. Students who reach a certain number of points can get a prize.

Structure of Classes

General structure of classes:

- Run solfege class once a week. Students may schedule an instrument lesson around solfege so they only have to come to the school once a week.

- Assuming four solfege classes in a month, the first three are "regular" classes where students solo their solfege number for the week, sing the next number assigned for next week with all students, and finish with ear training. The last class at the end of each month is music dictation, where students retrieve their dictation book, lapboard, and pencil to write down music an instructor plays.

- 45 minutes to 1 hour long depending on number of students and how advanced they are.

Two instructors are ideal, one to accompany and teach, and the other to walk the floor and stage to help students conduct time, keep track of where they are in the solfege book, and sing on pitch. During the ear training portion, the second instructor can guide students.

Students may play different instruments other than piano, and some may take solfege only. For those unfamiliar with a piano keyboard, a second instructor can orient them on *middle do*. Second instructors can orient new students privately while the class continues.

Considerations:

- Aggregate new students in groups of 3 - 5 so they're not singing alone.
    - If someone misses a week, makeup both songs next week.
    - For more significant absences, catch the group below. Students often have other interests - soccer, band, choir - and they sometimes rotate in and out.
- Disperse new students among more advanced students and have the advanced students watch/correct new ones, e.g. beating time.
- Once a year, consider a solfege concert somewhere (at a school, community center, church, senior center, etc). Note that preparation needed for this could take away from more ear training, for example. When I was a student at French School and Mlle. Combe was in her 80s, we prepared for piano recitals, not solfege recitals. The French School archives indicate that earlier generations did solfege recitals.

Structure of solfege classes

- Consider 30 minutes for beginner classes with younger students (five or below), 45 minutes to an hour for advanced and adult classes.
- Have each student solo the current assignment (marked at the end of the music with a diagonal, see image below on

the left). Once completed, cross through diagonal and mark next assignment (image below on the right). Award points based on how well they did.

- Discuss any new concepts in next number (e.g. introducing whole note/rest, half note/rest, dotted notes), then have the class sing the next number.

- If there is time, review the growing number of concepts.

- Finish with ear training.

Specific structure of dictation classes

- Students have their own dictation books.

- Teacher plays a melody.

- Students determine: what is the time signature? (How many beats per measure? The accompanist can firmly accent the first beat guiding students in correctly conducting the first down beat of every measure).

- Try to figure out if it's major or minor and what key it's in

- How many sharps or flats?

- Once the class has established the basics, start dictation on a new blank staff and write the clef, key signature, and time signature. The teacher then plays one bar at a time while students figure out the pitches and note durations. The most efficient system is to first write down the note heads, then the correct stems and a bar line.

- Once students have completed their work, the instructor reviews (or has advanced students compare their work in pairs and address discrepancies).

- Order: Treble clef, key signature (optional), time signature, notes / measures.

- Treble clef every line, key signature every line, time signature at the beginning (and if changed later)

Student Growth (long term)

1. Learn to sight sing while conducting time.

2. Learn dictation, develop the ear (ideally, absolute pitch)

3. Learn to sing without accompaniment (accompanist adapts to beginner / advanced students)

4. Learn how to lead the discussion for the next assignment by asking questions like: how many beats per measure?

5. Read bass clef

6. For piano students, learn to sightread treble and bass clef simultaneously for simple pieces

7. Add to knowledge of what the right questions are to ask: what is the pitch of the first note? What is the duration of the first note? Major, minor? Key signature?

8. Advanced students learn to coach less advanced counterparts. Coach advanced students to ask the right questions, instead of give the correct answers.

9. Begin learning how to compose music, and how to use solfege to learn to compose and improvise.

10. Accompany solfege class.

11. Go through this teaching guide, teach solfege classes, and mentor the next generation of teachers.

    ○ An important component of this for each new

generation is to have those trained in the French School method work with those who have spent a considerable amount of time learning piano without using the French School method (5 or more years). Search for people who have excellent critical thinking and communication skills who become wildly passionate about learning the French School method because they see the benefit. Those who are only familiar with the French School method can take its effectiveness for granted and be blind to exactly why each aspect of this methodology is so effective. The danger with this is that in teaching these methods to others, the effectiveness becomes watered down because the methods are applied within an incorrect paradigm.

- When working with those not trained in French School methods, think of the 30/30/30 rule. This is also a great guideline for navigating through life. Assume at every point in time, that you have 30% of the information, the other person has 30% of the information, there is an additional 30% of information that can only be uncovered when you collaborate with the other person. Finally, to get to 100%, there is 10% of the information that will never be discovered despite everyone's best efforts. What does this mean? Stay curious and adaptable.

Teacher Growth (long term)

1. Starting out: quick meeting at the end of each class to assess / refine

2. If things go well, transition to meeting monthly, then quarterly

3. Start with initial teachers, include advanced students-in-training later

4. Report on new findings (technologies, apps, music-as-a-business, social media, strategic partnerships with other art related organizations and the community, advocates, conservatories - e.g. Juilliard)

5. Learn to accompany and sing / talk simultaneously.

6. Learn to adapt accompaniment to students (add in melody? Have them sing acapella?).

Years ago when I worked in technology and branched into technical training, I took a Langevin Train the Trainer course. Two valuable quotes that came from this:

1. Learning is creation, not consumption.

2. Be the guide on the side, not the sage on the stage.

Also: show, don't tell.

Solfege Process Growth

By thinking in terms of "meta" levels, and coaching advanced students (e.g. the 11 year olds) on coaching their less advanced counterparts (e.g. the 7 year olds) on coaching their less advanced counterparts (e.g. the 5 year olds), the possibilities are endless and the knowledge space expands considerably - from learning about music, to also learning how to:

- learn,

- identify and solve problems,

- be efficient

- become a leader and influencer.

Running a Demonstration

Initial Preparation

- Recruit current piano/voice students and alumni/teachers willing to participate in a demonstration.

- Choose a popular number from the Dannhäuser solfege book to perform (e.g. 39).

- Learn the basics of singing and conducting 4/4 time

- Practice until all recruits are somewhat familiar with sight singing, singing on pitch, and conducting time. If they've never done this, this will take time to learn.

- Create an attendance sheet for audience members to give their name and phone number / email address, as well as list who might be interested in taking solfege.

- Create flyers announcing the demonstration.

Assure those who are concerned about the demo, that mistakes during the demo are OK. One of the most important things solfege students learn is how never to stop if they stumble, but to listen for the accompanist who may accent the downbeat so that they can conduct the first beat (down) and continue from there. Mistakes shouldn't be intentional during a demo but if they happen, they are part of the demo may ease recruits' performing concerns.

Lastly, make copies of solfege exercise one on card stock, and tape them to a board so that the audience members could each have a copy to place on their lap after the demo.

Structure of Solfege Demonstration

1. Give an introduction and some history, and explain to the local community the benefits of solfege.

2. Have solfege recruits come on stage, and place their solfege books on music stands around the piano.

3. Ask the audience: who is familiar with The Sound of Music? Raise your hand if you've heard of it. Many will raise their hands, which will make the demonstration that much easier since they already know how to solfege, they just might not realize it.

4. Sit at the piano, play middle do, and sing "do". Then play re, and sing "re"... and so on. Have the audience follow along. At "ti", explain that the French method is to use "si, a salty drink instead...". That's because historically, it was si before England introduced ti in the 19th century so that every note started with a different letter of the alphabet.

One note about using si: most Americans are familiar with the alphabetic notation for music - CDE instead of do re mi. Si and C sound exactly alike, but are different notes (because si is really B in alphabetic notation). Asking what the note is using alphabetic notation eliminates the confusion between si and C.

5. Introduce conducting 4/4 time, which looks like a cross. Make a fist with the right hand and hold the fist up (12 o'clock position). The first beat is down (6 o'clock position), second beat

is left (across the body at the 9 o'clock position), third beat is right (out at the 3 o'clock position), and fourth beat is up (12 o'clock position). Solfege demonstrators then demonstrate conducting time. Explain this isn't easy to do initially, and if people get lost, simply stop beating time, find where they are in the music, note where the other students are (the accompanist will often accent the downbeat), and catch up with the class on the next downbeat and continue.

6. Accompanist and demonstrators then demonstrate both exercise one, and whatever popular number they would like to perform.

7. After the demo, distribute solfege exercise one on card stock to the audience and have the audience learn to conduct time and sing the exercise. They will realize how challenging learning all of these things can be. This helps parents of prospective solfege students to develop some perspective and compassion for what their child will experience when starting out.

8. Remind the audience that if they haven't added their contact information to the attendance sheet, please do so. Once they walk out the door, it's impossible to contact them again.

Follow up after demonstration

Go through the attendance sheet, call / email attendees, thank them for attending, ask if they have any questions, and if there is interest, take further steps to enroll students into solfege.

Launching a New Class

Start solfege class at the beginning of the month, so that the first three (or four classes) are solfege and the last class of the month is dictation. This chapter addresses the logistics of launching a new class, but not the specific details. Those details come in the chapter titled *Foundation - Details*.

First Solfege Class

Have an attendance sheet for the first class and any time a new student starts to capture students' and parents' full names, and contact information. Pick up where the demo in the previous chapter leaves off.

If none of the students have done solfege before, they will be completely lost, which is normal. A brand new solfege class will be lost for about three classes before things start to click and they begin to catch on.

For the first class - introduce treble clef (also called the G clef), staff (with five lines and four spaces), and the notes. Since exercise one is a simple do major scale, think about The Sound of Music, look at the notes and also refer to the first page of Dannhäuser Solfège des Solfèges where the notes are written out: do re mi, etc.

Explain that the C shaped symbol they see at the beginning is used to denote 4/4 time (also called common time) and learn/review how to conduct 4/4 time.

Students new to conducting time consistently have trouble with the third beat. The third beat should be out to the right, at the 3 o'clock position. Newer students will often skip the third beat and go straight up to the fourth beat and lose track of time. Or their third beat is "lazy" and more down at the 5 o'clock position. Expect this in the beginning, and have them correct this sooner rather than later. That 3 o'clock position is also why folding chairs and stands need to be spaced appropriately so students can execute a third beat properly without hitting the person, cabinet, or wall to their right.

For very young students:

- If the instructor is facing the class and teaching students how to conduct time, the really young ones will raise the wrong hand. They haven't figured out spatial orientation yet, so face away from the class and demonstrate that conducting time is done with the right hand.

- Gauge their attention span. They may only be able to handle 15 minutes of solfege initially before they sit in back with a parent. This is also why we start with the youngest group.

Introduce whole notes, and that they have a duration of four beats. Introduce barlines, and that each bar has four beats, and the notes within each bar have to add up to four beats, so now we're also learning math!

Note the comma symbols - those are breath marks because singers can't keep singing without taking a breath.

Sing exercise 1 while conducting time. The accompanist plays, and one or two assistants are walking on the floor to ensure students:

- pay attention, focus on the music, and know where they are in the music (point if necessary using a pencil). Students who can't sightread well often look at the accompanist for reassurance, instead of their music.

- beat time correctly. Assistants/accompanist will need to

correct students periodically or say "down" to indicate the first beat

- sight sing the correct notes

For a brand new class, almost no one will sing, or they'll sing very quietly. It's a foreign class, and they're surrounded by strangers. That won't last for long. By the third class, even normally shy kids will have bonded and the class will start getting noisy.

Notes for the accompanist:

Here is the accompaniment music for exercise one:

Play accompaniment with the melody as whole notes and the rest of the notes played as repeated quarter notes. Why?

- New students will struggle with sight singing while conducting time. Having a constant quarter note beat helps students keep better track of time when learning how to conduct 4/4 time. Clearly accent the first beat and remind students when they hear that, move their right fist down. Call out "down!" when playing the first beat if necessary.

- This small change, plus the slow tempo (Lento) of exercise one, turns this exercise into a regal march. And there is no better way to celebrate a new student's entry into the world of solfege, than with a regally performed exercise 1.

- To start each exercise, play the first chord so students hear the pitch, count 1, 2, ready, go! Then play and have students sing together. For students working to develop absolute pitch, have them hum the starting note they will sing first, then play the first chord. Students will then begin conducting time and sync up.

By the third week, students will understand the structure of solfege class. Have assistants evaluate progress, and if necessary, repeat the first three exercises until students are more comfortable. Laying a solid foundation in the early days is important. The second exercise will throw them off because of the half notes, and the fact that new students tend to have trouble with the third beat. After the first three exercises, jump straight to 11. Exercises 4 - 10 cover the intervals, and rather than go through these, ear training covers learning the intervals. By jumping straight to 11, students immediately begin singing real songs.

From exercise 11 on, establish a blueprint for how to evaluate new music by asking:

- How many beats per measure?

- (For newer students) How do we beat time?

- What is the pitch of the first note? (Do, re, mi, etc.)

- (Advanced students: hum the first note before the accompanist plays anything)

- What is the duration of the first note? (Whole note, half note, etc.) Beat one may start with a rest.

Progress through the exercises and award points depending on how well students do. The point is not to perfect the exercises, that's what instrument lessons are for. The point of solfege, week after week, is to introduce students to a new exercise they've never seen before and have them learn to quickly break it down and sightread it. Because new students start periodically, and a class may have several small groups assigned a different exercise - that's where students will get their repetition, since the entire class sings the next number to be assigned for the next week. If students can't continue until they have perfected an exercise, they might tune out, and this defeats the primary purpose of solfege - learning how to sightread new music.

This will usually take about 30 minutes. Assuming a 45 minute class, leave the last 15 minutes for individual students to sit at the second piano and do ear training. Because they're new, start with do, re, mi. Start with middle do, so that they can orient. Students who are not taking piano lessons will need to be shown middle do. Have them figure out do, re, fa. Initially they'll have a lot of trouble. Prompt by asking did this note go up or down? Discourage them from guessing and slamming random notes. Ask them to listen to the note and think about it before playing the keyboard. Accuracy is more important than speed. New students tend to have more trouble with descending notes, as opposed to ascending, both in terms of sight singing, and ear training. There will be further detailed discussion on ear training later.

Because one student at a time goes up to the second piano, the rest of the class can get unruly, which is understandable. Assistants can keep newer students engaged with questions like: "can you identify this note"? For the more advanced students, come armed with training games like:

Quiz

Have the advanced students brainstorm three questions to ask the beginner students. They could go to the chalkboard, draw a note, and ask what the note is. Or ask what the duration is, etc.

Which is False?

Advanced students come up with three statements, and beginner students have to figure out which of the three is invalid. Examples: a whole note has 3 beats. Draw middle do on a chalkboard and label it re. Draw an eighth rest and say it's a quarter rest.

The statements could even be bars of music. Examples: a 4/4 bar with a dotted half note and half note. A 2/4 bar with a whole note.

There is a set of sample exercises at the end of this book that can be distributed to the class to work on while other groups are singing or students are doing ear training. The class won't be any quieter, but they will be fully engaged.

After a new group has completed three or four solfege classes and is starting to gel - pull the rug out from under their feet. The last class of the month will be their first dictation class.

First Dictation Class

Normal solfege classes are analogous to teaching someone how to drive a car. Learning to write music is analogous to teaching someone how to become an auto mechanic. Learning to read music involves learning about note pitches and durations, rests, etc.

A student trying to figure out a piece of music and write it down must be able to determine how many beats per measure, conduct it, identify if the song starts on the first beat, figure out the pitches, the durations, and where the barlines go. Students learn for a four beat bar, a whole note can fit in that bar, or two half notes, or four quarter notes, or a half note and two quarter notes, or two quarter notes and a half note...

This hacks the brain at a very deep level in terms of understanding music, and ties together everything students started to learn in their regular solfege classes. When the instructor plays a bar of music and the class has to figure out the pitches - that's ear training. When students have figured out the pitches and have to conduct time to determine the duration of those notes, this reinforces conducting time.

The first thing new students need to learn is how to draw a treble clef.

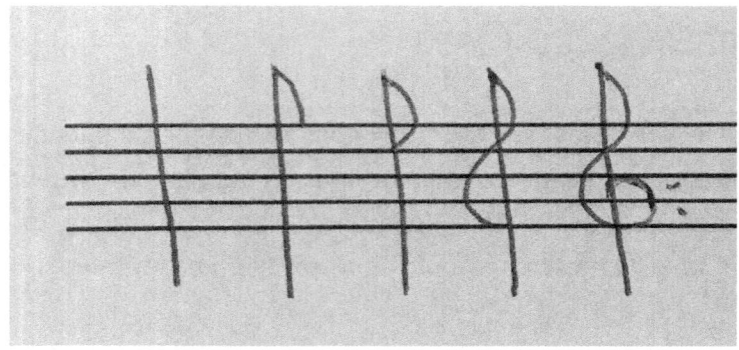

Draw this on the board and have students draw an entire line of treble clefs. Check after they've done three treble clefs, make corrections, then have them continue. Have them do a second line if it's necessary. For truly young students (age 5 or younger) this is really tough.

Truly young students may be a bit discouraged initially because everyone around them is so much bigger and knows so much more. Maybe older students are already doing fractions in school so some concepts are easier for them. But younger students are getting an earlier start, and that early start is priceless.

New dictation students must learn to write the time signature, and then notes, starting with middle do. Show them how to write whole notes, half notes, quarter notes, and eighth notes. Repeat writing do a couple times, then re, up to the do one octave up. Then write a couple lines of middle do high do, middle do high do. Then re and high re, up to mi and high mi. Learn to write the rests, and the difference between handwritten quarter rests and eighth rests. This covers the first dictation class.

After the basics, they're ready to begin to figure out and write down what an instructor plays.

Have students start each new dictation assignment on a new staff, and place their treble clef and time signature. Subsequent lines will need a new treble clef but not the time signature. Show them how to end their exercise with a double bar. Other useful information to include: initials and a date.

Joining an Existing Class

Throw them in. An infant comes into this world not knowing how to speak, and one day, assuming their hearing works and they are surrounded by speaking adults, they simply begin to speak. All that is necessary is to immerse them in a speaking environment. Solfege works the same way, because from day one students begin creating and understanding music. They will be lost initially, but they'll have more advanced classmates they can watch. Intersperse new students among the older students so that the older students can correct things like conducting time.

This is also where the assistants are vital - for very young students they can spend the time during the first class giving a new student private instruction on the notes and durations, etc.

Teenage / Adult Students

Set up a separate class where older students are on equal footing age/skill-wise. Adult classes tend to be inconsistent because work schedules may interfere. Instead of going through one exercise a week, individual adult students will randomly choose and go through three exercises a week, meaning the class could sing 10 different exercises or more.

In addition to sightreading training, older students generally have trouble singing on pitch, so going through exercises forcing them to sing acapella is helpful. Watch for the tendency to sing descending notes with too great an interval so that at the end they are flat.

A serious note to prospective parents with no musical background: at minimum, consider taking solfege lessons. This will enable you to accurately assess the effectiveness of music instructors for your children. Even if you yourself may not become a self-sufficient musician, giving the next generation the greatest possible chance for success with music will not only yield better musicians, studies show this actively affects brain intelligence. The information in the Background section detailing how the lives of French School alumni have unfolded over these decades bears this out. Also, read the chapter titled "Mozart Effect DIY Kit".

Taking A Step Back

What makes this solfege methodology effective?

Unlike private instrument lessons, solfege is a class. By externalizing everything, students have no place to hide. They know something or they don't, and it becomes clear to everyone immediately - students, parents and teachers.

- Singing on pitch or off pitch?

- Using the correct solfege names for each pitch? Is do really do? Or did a student say do when singing re?

- Conducting time correctly? With a class it's easy to identify someone who is out of sync.

- Two piano ear training accurate or hunting and pecking?

While this can be intimidating initially - having no place to hide - students often discover everyone has different strengths and areas to work on. Different strengths will require students to build different sets of skills to become self-sufficient musicians:

- Those with absolute pitch will usually be able to memorize music quickly and can perform memorized music. This may be a challenge to developing good sightreading skills.

- Those unable to develop a good ear will need to develop excellent sightreading skills. They will tend to perform with music (which can serve as a safety net against memory blanks).

By externalizing everything that is important to understanding music, the French School solfege methodology not only teaches music fundamentals, it serves as a diagnostic tool for teachers.

The piano accompaniment provides students with a framework. That framework is pretty solid initially, but even by exercise 14 there are sections where students will begin to sing acapella. If students are doing well, let them sing those areas acapella. If they are having trouble singing on-pitch, also play the melody. If students go off pitch, repeat the melody note several times and focus their attention on it. This helps them learn to sing on-pitch over time.

Administrative Considerations

Reminder: Capture contact information for all students.

Consider having parents sign an agreement before classes start, that they will pay a monthly fee for solfege due the first of the month. The fee is paid regardless of whether students attend or not. Set the correct expectations up front.

When several of us initially rebooted solfege classes, one member would email a write up every week of each student's strengths/weaknesses and progress. This was incredibly helpful. Here are some of the things we caught in those early classes:

- Name of each student so that we could begin calling them by name, plus their ages

- What kind of musical experience they have (can they read music?), what instrument do they play?

- Was the length of the class appropriate for the number of students?

- Was the breakdown of the class appropriate, e.g. enough time to sing the numbers and do ear training?

- Age ranges - if the range is too great, do we run two 45 minute classes back to back? One for young students, and one for older students / adult students?

New Solfege Instructors

Ideally, solfege instructors should have absolute pitch or *absolute relative pitch* and be good sight readers (given a starting pitch, a person with absolute relative pitch becomes indistinguishable from someone with absolute pitch. A background in music composition will make music dictation classes that much more effective.

Accompanists should be able to play and sing/teach simultaneously. For those who have never done this, this can be challenging. Another neat skill to learn: play the melody with your left hand while beating time with your right hand, and sight singing the notes.

Those who compose will learn that they can adapt the accompaniments on-the-fly, which is useful because accompanists can then:

- play something simpler and pay more attention to what is going on with the class.

- incorporate the melody in case a student is having trouble singing on key.

- make the same exercise sound different, so that students aren't relying on the accompaniment for cues.

Don't let students strain their voices if the notes go too high. For students who are inexperienced singers, or male students whose voices are changing, tell them they can sing an octave lower if needed, until they get back in range.

Students will stumble right and left. Never stop playing the first time around. Learning how to barrel through mistakes is learning how to be a professional musician. A Juilliard string quartet sightreading compositions for the first time can run into any number of challenges if a composer's sheet music isn't crystal clear. Do they stop and say "oh, sorry!" Absolutely not. They barrel through as best they can unless they totally, completely fall apart or the professor stops them. If everyone said "oh, sorry!" every time they made a mistake, everyone would have to stop and regroup. That's valuable time wasted in a 20 minute reading where performers sightread and play while composers record the performance.

Conduct solfege classes in the same spirit, and only when the exercise is complete, review any challenging areas or concepts. Students will need to learn:

- If they stumble while singing, stop singing but keep following along in the music and pick up

- If they stumble while conducting time, stop conducting and wait for the next first beat

When students are standing, have them place their left hand behind their back. That way the arm isn't dangling or wiggling around, and it supports better posture when standing. Don't have them place their left hand behind their back when they are sitting, because they need to hold their solfege book on their laps. Discourage students from beating time by tapping their feet. While tapping the foot is another way of keeping time, it does not tell you which beat, whereas conducting time does.

Mozart Effect DIY Kit

Start a musical education before a child is born. A segue into our family history will both shed light and dispel myths.

We moved to Plainfield, NJ when I was two years old, and learned about The French School of Music when I was seven. Dad's boss had two daughters who were taking piano lessons at French School.

Dad took seven years of piano lessons with a mediocre piano teacher and struggled to reach an intermediate level, and before we were born, sis and I listened to him practicing Beethoven sonatas. As a graduate student at Cornell who was strapped for cash, he taught himself to tune a piano.

We have silent family video of my playing piano as a toddler, with a children's songbook on the piano stand. Mom taught me what she could. From dad's stories, she would try to teach me to read music, but I was too slow to respond so she would show me the notes. I must have learned to play by ear for five years.

When I started piano and solfege at French School, Mlle. Combe quickly determined I had absolute pitch. My three year old sister sat in back of the solfege class with mom.

One day during ear training, she asked mom: "why can't he get those? Those are so *easy!*" One of the mothers sitting in front of her turned around and looked at her in complete shock. She told Mlle. Combe, who stopped the solfege class and asked my sister to come up.

Mlle. Combe started doing simple ear training with single notes, and my sister got them. Then she tried a few more things, and my sister got them. She kept trying more complicated things, and my sister kept getting them! Practically the next week, my sister started piano and solfege lessons. She gave her first French School recital at age 4 1/2.

This would seem to be a mystery. Our dad was a mediocre pianist who back then was uninformed about the French School method. Neither of my parents had absolute pitch, so it's not like it was obvious there was some genetic component that we were "born" with. I am not a molecular geneticist and the field of epigenetics with respect to music is likely in its infancy, but the right environment and the French School solfege method taught at an early age could very well be strong epigenetic influences.

If dad had sat down and mangled a couple of Beethoven sonatas for Mlle. Combe, she would have said "oh, of course, this was inevitable." But he never did so she never knew. Had she ever come to our house, she would have realized our piano was tuned, and that dad tuned the piano regularly.

Anyone who wants to give their child the greatest possible musical head start in life must do something similar. Today, electronic pianos don't have to be tuned. If parents don't play, they can listen to classical music by Mozart, Beethoven, Bach, etc. and attend concerts.

One last story: A woman living in our building has two sons. The older son went to Cornell, and the younger one gravitated toward music. She asked: why doesn't my first son like music but my second son does?

In two minutes we determined her first son had no problems falling asleep at night. The younger son could never fall asleep so even though she's not a musician, she started singing to him so he would fall asleep.

What myths did this dispel?

"Geniuses" aren't "born" - well, they kind of are, but not in the way many might think. The foundation building blocks are created when the child is immersed in the right conditions early. This doesn't happen without intent, the "affinity" is really a skill that must be cultivated like any other skill.

The earlier you start, the better. If you want your children to have a chance of developing absolute pitch, set them up for success by exposing them to:

- in tune music before they are born
- only tuned instruments

Why are tuned instruments so important? Because if they are not tuned, even those with a predisposition towards developing absolute pitch will be the last to think they have absolute pitch. It would be like teaching them to add, subtract, multiply and divide in octal, then letting them loose in the real world. They will think they are math idiots.

The best way to develop absolute pitch is to focus first on one pitch: middle do. Start by listening intently to the pitch for middle do. Then, try thinking of a middle do before playing middle do (on a pitch pipe, instrument, or any of the online bootcamp exercises). Do this long enough and at some point you will tune in. By practicing the intervals, you can then tune into any other pitch. Graduate to regularly practicing both do and sol, without relying on intervals. Achieve absolute pitch with all of the notes in the do major scale first, then add the sharps and flats later.

Foundation - Details

Now that solfege class has launched, the rest of the chapters in this guide will cover:

- Further details of each of the main areas of solfege, using the French School method

- Using this foundation to learn how to improvise and compose

- Key concepts in piano practice that dovetail with solfege

- How this foundation together with music related apps and technology lead to infinite possibilities

- Additional topics to help solfege students prepare for a conservatory environment

The goal is for students to develop a consistent level of competency with respect to the fundamentals such that they are self-sufficient enough to continue broadening and deepening their understanding of music.

Sight Singing

In the nineteenth century, Anglophone countries like Britain changed si to ti so that each note started with a different syllable. This makes it possible to solfege the chromatic scale with raised pitches (sharps) by using do, di (for do sharp), re, ri, mi, fa, fi, so, si, la, li, ti and do. The syllables for the flats are do, ti, te, la, le, so, se, fa, mi, me, re, ra, do. Changing si to ti means there is no ambiguity with the chromatic syllables for sol and si. The French method entails singing do re mi, and re could be re, re#, or re♭ depending on the key. There are pros and cons to each system.

French method:

- Even young children can pick this up easily, there are only seven syllables to learn.

- Instructors can clearly hear every syllable (do re mi etc.)

- Do begins with a hard percussive consonant, and so does ti. But si is softer and more lyrical.

- There are times you may want a do♭, which is si. This system allows you to sing do (for do♭) even though the pitch is si.

Changing si to ti and adding chromatic syllables facilitates greater awareness of the chromatic scale and the enharmonic equivalents.

Check the *References* section at the end of this guide for downloadable handouts for drilling students in the basics.

Basic singing techniques:

- Stand straight, like a puppet being pulled up on a string at the top of your head. This is different from the military stance of "chin up, chest out, shoulders back, and stomach in"

- Breathe from your stomach, not high up in your chest which can constrict your throat

- Yawn - do you feel how the space right behind your nose opens up? Singing should feel like this

Sightreading

Drill the notes with flash cards and the solfege book so they become automatic. Younger students may require separate one-on-one attention for this.

A tip for mastering intervals is associating intervals with well-known songs:

- Minor second - Jaws
- Major second - Happy Birthday
- Minor third - Greensleeves
- Major third - When the Saints Go Marching In
- Perfect fourth - Here Comes the Bride
- Tritone - Maria
- Perfect fifth - Twinkle Twinkle Little Star
- Minor sixth - The Entertainer
- Major sixth - My Bonnie Lies Over the Ocean
- Minor seventh - Somewhere
- Major seventh - Take On Me
- Octave - Somewhere Over the Rainbow

At the end of solfege exercise 23, introduce the sharps and flats (using the French method, this is a lyrical jingle):

- Sharps: fa do sol re la mi si

- Flats: si mi la re sol do fa

Break the sequence up like a phone number so it is easier to learn and remember:

fa do sol - re la mi si

si mi la - re sol do fa

These jingles makes figuring out key signatures easy.

For major scales with sharp key signatures, take the last sharp and go up one note. Three sharps? fa do sol. Take sol, go up one note, the key is la major.

la si do# re mi fa# sol# la

For major scales with flat key signatures, go back one flat. Two flats? si mi. The key is si♭ major.

si♭ do re mi♭ fa sol la si♭

Practice engaging in musical mental play to hear these scales on pitch without a keyboard and without singing.

At exercise 67, introduce bass clef (exercise 147). Do a few exercises in bass clef, return to treble, and alternate back and forth. Tell students to take the note in treble clef and go up two notes, until reading bass clef becomes second nature.

Tips and tricks for more effective sightreading:

- Before the accompanist starts playing, look at the music - how many beats per measure? What is the key signature? Which notes will be sharp/flat? What are the first few pitches? What types of notes are they (e.g. quarter rest followed by quarter note, dotted quarter and eighth…) Mentally play this in your head.

- Once the accompanist starts playing, continue looking ahead. Looking ahead increases the chance of figuring out the music before you actually have to sing it. During page turns, those who look ahead already know what to sing and can turn the page and read what comes next, without stopping.

Cleartune App

Search online for the Cleartune mobile app, which is only available on the App Store for iOS devices (Apple). This can be a useful tool for practicing solfege. After installing the app, click on the information button in the lower right corner. This displays the Settings, like Calibration, Temperament, etc. Tap the Notation setting, and select Fixed Do Solfege (choose sharp or flat depending on preference). Return to Settings, then tap Done to return to the main screen, which will now display a wheel with the solfege notes. Take one of the solfege numbers, and sing the solfege notes slowly and clearly. The Cleartune app will swivel with each note, showing the solfege note. This will allow students to validate two things: the pitch, and that they are using the correct name for each pitch. This is a sensitive app, so if you breathe the wheel will spin to the pitch it detects. Also, it's accuracy has fluctuated at times depending on changes to the iOS mobile operating system.

2-Hand Tapping

Once students can sight sing a melody, how can they practice sightreading multiple lines of music simultaneously and coordinating different rhythms using two hands, the way a pianist would? Search for William Wieland's website and 2-Hand Tapping. He has webpages with rhythms for right and left hand that start with quarter notes and quarter rests that become progressively more advanced.

The Absolute Pitch Loophole

Those who have absolute pitch and memorize music quickly by ear may have trouble practicing sightreading. They will memorize all of the solfege exercises as soon as they hear them. For more advanced students practicing piano sightreading, go through a book of Mozart sonatinas quickly. Short simpler exercises from Le Carpentier (now out of print), Le Couppey, Burgmuller, and Czerny are good for sightreading practice.

Where students are advanced both in solfege and piano, tap them as solfege accompanists for more sightreading training.

Instructors and advanced students who compose can compose solfege exercises for the entire class to sightread cold.

Conducting Time

Students make a fist with their right hand. If they're standing, the left hand goes behind their back, otherwise if they're sitting, the left hand holds their solfege book while they beat time with their right hand.

Beating time:

- 4 beats per measure: shape is a cross, down, left across the body, out to the right, and up

- 3 beats looks like a triangle: down, out to the right (3 o'clock), and up

- 2 beats looks like a straight line: down, then up

- C with line through is cut-time, also four beats but two down, then two up

- 6 beats: three down, then three up

- 5 beats looks like a triangle with 3 beats, followed by 2 beats down and up

When students understand how to beat time for the current assignment, mention the bottom number in a time signature.

- C means 4/4 - four beats per measure, where a quarter note gets one beat. This is also known as common time.

- 3/4 - three beats per measure, a quarter note gets one beat.

- 3/8 - three beats per measure, an eighth note gets one beat (exercise 71 in Dannhäuser).

For Dannhäuser Book 1, the time signatures are mostly basic. 6/8 isn't introduced until almost the end.

Download the handouts mentioned in the *References* section as teaching aids.

Triplets are introduced in exercise 76. Ask students:

- Why do you need 3 for the triplet?

- What is the difference between a triplet and three eighth notes?

Because conducting 4/4 time shows the quarter note beats but not eighth note beats, teach students how to count those out loud at first, then in their head:

- Eighth notes: 1 and 2 and 3 and 4 and

- Triplets: 1 and and 2 and and 3 and and 4 and and

- Sixteenth notes: 1 and and and 2 and and and 3 and and and 4 and and and

Also note that they have the same number of beats per measure, whether they are counted

1 2 3 4

or 1 and 2 and 3 and 4 and

For advanced students, cover the triplet / duplet pattern by having students tap out a triplet several times with their right hand, then a duplet several times with their left hand.

Teaching aids while tapping this pattern out include "hot cup of tea" or "together, right left right" (or left right left).

The triplet / duplet pattern is fascinating because it alternates between both hands being on the beat, and then alternating (right left right or left right left). If it were always off the beat, it would be chaos. And if it were always on the beat it would be completely stable. But because the pattern alternates between on the beat and off the beat, it feels as if it waddles like a penguin.

Debussy's first Arabesque is a good triplet / duplet demonstration to show how the pattern works in music (play this slow first, then faster).

Ear Training

This is how two piano ear training progresses over time. Keep in mind this will be harder for students who don't take piano lessons.

Single notes, always start with middle do.

For all new students doing ear training for the first time, determine if they can discern between pitches going up versus going down. Start off sequentially (do, re, mi, re, mi, fa, sol).

Then jump an occasional note to see if students can discern between different simple intervals: do, re, fa, mi, sol, la, sol, mi, re…

Short sequences

If they are proficient with single notes, progress to short sequences. Don't jump more than one note initially, and progress as they develop competence.

Do re mi. Re mi fa. Mi do re. Etc.

Intervals

Return to two note sequences, and specifically bring their attention to simple white key intervals initially, both identifying the interval and playing the interval. Also begin to test their ability to discern larger intervals (sixth, seventh, on up).

Then test their ability to recognize intervals as two note chords. Play chords and return to the sequence of notes if they are having trouble hearing the individual notes when a chord is played. Have the class identify the interval for the sequence and/or chord.

Initially, stay with middle do as the bottom note, until they recognize those intervals. Keep in mind, students who play instruments that generate a single note (clarinet, saxophone) may have more trouble discerning chords during ear training. They should still learn to recognize intervals, however. Students who play an instrument like guitar may recognize and even develop absolute pitch for some chords more easily than others depending on their repertoire.

Start testing for absolute pitch

Determine if students can identify a note that is not automatically middle do. It could be re or mi. If they consistently say do, re, and mi correctly, branch to fa and sol, etc.

Sing base note and interval

Give students a base note and an interval in the do major scale. The instructor can optionally play the bottom note, and have them sing the two notes before playing the notes on the piano keyboard. Example:

Instructor: do sixth

Student: sings do la, then plays the notes

Single notes jumping around in compound intervals

This is about seeing both if students are becoming acclimated to knowing pitches *and* pitch classes, not just figuring out the next note in ear training based on simple intervals (in other words, we went up a third, down a fifth). For example, play middle do, then la two octaves above. Teach students to go up or down octaves for one of the notes to identify the interval. When hearing two notes played in quick succession, students can learn what a fourth is. But play one note, then wait, and play another, and suddenly the student may not be able to tell what is going on.

Top or bottom?

Continue testing intervals in the do major scale but now crawling up and down the keyboard. Start with middle do and sol.

Then change only one note at a time - it could be the top or the bottom note. Prompt the students with: "top or bottom?" and have them figure out two things:

> A. Did the top or bottom note change?
>
> B. How did that note change? Did it go up or down on the keyboard?

Even for more advanced students, they'll initially determine that the top or or bottom note changed, but they'll have trouble figuring out if that note went up or down. Here is an example sequence of chords (separate the notes if students are having trouble with chords initially):

> Do sol, do la, re la, re sol, mi sol, mi si, mi do, mi re…

Continue testing with a combination of two piano ear training, plus having students sing intervals. Each method teaches something different. Two piano ear training tests students' ability to hear chords - multiple notes that sound simultaneously. Having students sing a base note with two, three, and four note sequences tests their ability to engage in mental play and know what pitches they intend to produce, without relying on the piano.

Familiar songs

There are any number of children's songs which are ideal and fun for ear training, by playing a small phrase at a time:

- Alphabet song
- Itsy Bitsy Spider
- Old MacDonald Had a Farm
- Take Me Out to the Ballgame
- London Bridge
- Mary Had a Little Lamb
- Yankee Doodle
- You Are My Sunshine
- This Old Man
- Ten In A Bed
- Twinkle Twinkle

- Happy Birthday
- Rock-a-Bye Baby
- On Top of Spaghetti
- Three Blind Mice
- Frere Jacques (canon)
- How Much is that Doggy in the Window?
- She'll be Coming Round the Mountain When She Comes
- The Surprise

Chromatic scale

Once students become advanced enough in these basics, add in first do sharp and re sharp until students become proficient. Then add the rest of the sharps. Revisit some of the above exercises like top or bottom, adding in chromatic notes. Continue to do both two piano training as well as having them sing the notes before playing them on a keyboard. Refine their understanding of intervals - instead of simple intervals in do major, now introduce major / minor, augmented / diminished, tritone, etc.

Transposing

Review the sharps and flats regularly, then see if they can figure out each scale.

Take each phrase of some of the popular songs above, and keep switching keys.

> We Wish You a Merry Christmas:
>
> do fa - fa sol fa mi re, re
>
> mi la - la si la sol fa#, re
>
> si mi - mi fa mi re do, la
>
> mi♭ mi♭ fa, si♭, sol, la♭...

Extra credit: what key was each phrase in?

Interesting Rhythms

Play with the seventh chord and add interesting rhythms:

One and two And three and Four and Five and have them play variations like:

> do mi sol si (for the first bar, using the rhythm above)
>
> do mi sol la (for the second bar, back to...)
>
> do mi sol si (for the third bar)
>
> do mi♭ sol si

And repeat the pattern. Then go up to re fa la do, using the same rhythm, and from there have students begin improvising their own variations. If a friend plays the saxophone, they can now improvise an accompaniment for the saxophonist and have an informal jam session.

At this point some students are advanced enough to add in trills or grace notes. As students progress, lengthen the segments used for ear training.

R2D2

Students should be fairly proficient with three and four note chords before teachers can go R2D2 on them jumping around on the keyboard with completely atonal sequences and dissonant chords.

Some Considerations

In the early 20th century the US standardized A, or la, at 440 Hz, when previous tunings included 432 and 435 Hz. Given today's technology, it's easy for people to chose their own tuning. Different genres like house and techno often slide notes, or flatten the bass while simultaneously sharpening the melody. These are cool effects, and, this can impact a student's ability to develop and maintain absolute pitch.

While ear training will help students develop the best ear that they can have, not everyone will develop absolute pitch (roughly half of our solfege class in the 1970s either had absolute pitch or were no more than half step off in either direction). The end goal is to be able to write down something composed in your head. If what you composed was really in the key of fa, and it was notated in the key of mi, simply transpose the entire thing later.

What is really important is to develop accuracy with the intervals. If there is a sequence of notes going up and the middle note is a do and that same note occurs on the way down, it should still be a do, the ear shouldn't shift in the middle such that the listener now thinks it's a do# or re, because this makes it more difficult if not impossible to capture sheet music accurately.

Sight singing the notes correctly in fixed do doesn't just mean sightreading the notes correctly, but when doing mental play, no slippage occurs either up or down when running through a particular song, in the way the general public has trouble with the Happy Birthday song:

> Happy Birthday to you,
>
> Happy Birthday to you,
>
> Happy Birth —

This is an octave jump, and most people aren't accurate for one of two reasons:

1. the starting pitch was too high and most people can't physically sing the higher note

2. they can't accurately gauge an octave interval

The bottom line is that once they've made that incorrect jump, they're in a completely different key, and because there is generally a group of people singing, everybody is in a completely different key.

If students have had considerable ear training, and still absolute pitch in a fixed do system is not possible or accurate, at least have absolute relative pitch down cold.

Synesthesia

Those who have synesthesia experience cross-wired senses. For example, hearing the note re or something raspy may be accompanied by the color blue. Check the section titled Synesthesia for an interview with my brother-in-law who has synesthesia.

Proprioception

Proprioception may provide yet another source of information when developing or maintaining absolute pitch, e.g. when singing. As a first soprano, when I sing the second sol higher than middle do, this is the first note where I am forced to open my sinuses and sing from higher up in my head as opposed to down in my throat.

The downside of relying on proprioception as a singer gauging the feel of vocal chords occurs if you have surgery, e.g. to remove a thyroid lobe or goiter. In my case, had I not had absolute pitch just from an audio-centric standpoint, a reliance on proprioception would have thrown my skills out the window. When doing ear training, consider using proprioception as an additional information vector, and a temporary stepping stone to attaining true absolute pitch.

Losing Pitch: Research

For many years, I had a Sonicare toothbrush that would vibrate at middle do. When it finally broke, I bought another one, and discovered it vibrated smack between si and do! It took about four weeks before my sense of pitch started to waver. First it became difficult distinguishing between si and do. Then si flat, si, and do. Then I realized I was starting to have trouble distinguishing the fifth interval (do sol). I ditched the Sonicare toothbrush and went with Oral-B, because it vibrates in a more diffused noise, as opposed to a more directed pitch.

Build a Solfege Playlist

If you have the ability to access audio files directly, find songs that you enjoy, and alter the filenames by inserting the name of the starting pitch before the title of the song. Use a pitch pipe to make sure the pitch is accurate! Put your playlist on shuffle and see if you can identify the starting note. As you become more advanced, see how many more notes you can identify in the melody, and how quickly. Try both singing the notes and engaging in mental play as you listen.

We live in a world filled with music that pitch bends. We can also recalibrate our hearing daily with short exercises and a solfege playlist.

Music Dictation

At the start of class, students will need to retrieve their dictation book, as well as a lapboard and pencil. Make sure there are plenty of erasers.

The instructor can compose something on the spot for dictation based on what the class needs. Other ideas for dictation:

- Use a familiar song like Twinkle Twinkle (students have fun figuring out familiar tunes)
- Take solfege exercises in bass clef, and have students transpose to treble clef or vice versa

Have students transpose a familiar song like Twinkle Twinkle in several different keys.

Starting a Dictation Session

- Play a song, accenting the first beat of each measure.
- Have students conduct time and figure out how many beats per measure.

For beginner students, pick / compose songs that:

- Start on the first beat
- Are in do major
- Use whole notes down to eighth notes, including dotted quarter notes

Work bar by bar. Play the notes for each bar and have students solfege the notes using their ear training. Have them put the note heads down on paper with the correct pitches.

Then have them conduct time to figure out the timing of each bar, and add the correct type of note. Use pencils so that they can erase and change noteheads (e.g. from quarter to half when they beat time and realize the duration is a half note).

Explain the importance of knowing the time signature and how many beats go into a bar. Have students work out some different options that could work for a 4/4 bar:

- 1 whole note (or 1 whole rest)
- 2 half notes (or 1 half note, 1 half rest, etc.)
- 1 half note, 2 quarter notes
- Dotted half note, quarter note
- 4 quarter notes
- Etc.

When students cover the sharps and flats, have them write them in their dictation book:

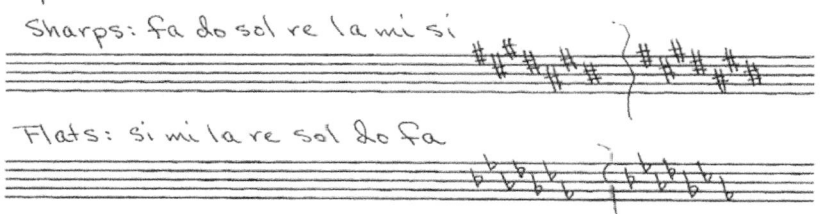

Questions in the form of brain teasers can be fun:

- Can a whole note fit into a 3/4 bar? If not, what can fit into a 3/4 bar?

- Here is a 4/4 bar with a half note. What kinds of notes or rests can you use to complete this bar?

For more advanced sessions:

- Introduce pickup bars and have students try to figure out on which beat the music starts. A pickup bar includes the notes that are played, not the rests in front.

- Choose different keys and have students determine what key the music is in, whether it's major or minor, and what the key signature is

- Add sixteenth notes, triplets, and dotted eighth / sixteenth combinations

- Compose a shorter section of music, and have students come up with lyrics and learn to notate lyrics in music

Considerations

While many people use music notation software like Sibelius, Finale, and Dorico (or even free software like MuseScore), music dictation classes must always start with learning to write music by hand.

When students are well-versed in handwritten music dictation, introduce them to free music notation software like MuseScore.

This could be a stepping stone to Sibelius, Finale, or Dorico later if they become serious composers.

Improving Solfege Skills

Having established how solfege works, what skills do students need to continue improving their solfege skills? The answer is to draw on French School piano practice techniques and adapt them to the solfege world.

This is just a cursory treatment of these methods. For more information, check my dad's book *Fundamentals of Piano Practice*.

Continuity Rule

While the goal of solfege is to learn to approach a new piece of music and systematically break it down, these skills don't become automatic without practice. Efficient piano practice when learning difficult pieces involves breaking music into short segments, and using a technique called the *continuity rule*. Practice one bar of music plus the next note with one hand, repeatedly, until the segment can be played multiple times in a row proficiently. Then move to the next bar plus the next note and repeat the process until comfortable. Return to the first bar plus the next note (which you have likely forgotten). Practice again to regain proficiency, and repeat until each bar plus the next note can be played. Then string them together - practice two bars plus the next note. Work on the third bar, then string together the second and third bars, review first and second, then string together first, second and third bars plus the next note.

The continuity rule ensures that practice overlaps the music in a comprehensive way so that students can eventually play a complicated passage without stopping. Challenging passages require the same targeted focus - one bar at a time plus the next note, and stringing those bars into larger segments, until those areas can be played proficiently. If the passage is so challenging students can only handle half a bar, practice half a bar plus the next note.

This efficient method can be applied to solfege as well. For example, here is a tongue twister that is challenging to sing quickly:

fa la re fa mi sol do mi fa re do si do mi do

Break this down in a similar manner starting slowly: fa la re fa mi, and repeat until comfortable.

Then mi sol do mi fa (note the repeated last note from the first pattern). Now string them together. Then try speeding this up, breaking down any problem areas.

This is a great way to identify problem areas and common patterns and practice them. When encountering another new piece of music with similar types of patterns, the brain is liable to break them down during a sightreading session much more quickly.

While the continuity rule is by far the most powerful tool in the French School arsenal, there is one important caveat with respect to using the continuity rule when practicing piano, regarding fingering. It's possible for some musical passages to have multiple valid options for fingering, but in order to maximally focus on technique, musicality, and memorization, it is vital to choose one specific fingering. Otherwise, performers will always require some form of conscious thought when playing because it won't be completely imbued within the muscle memory. When using the continuity rule, it is equally vital for the pianist to know what was going on in the previous passage, coming into the current passage. Know what the correct fingering is, otherwise you risk using the continuity rule to practice the wrong fingering. This is especially true when pianists may change what is written because they found a more comfortable solution or they have small hands. Ensure any changes in fingering are clearly documented.

While it may seem that using the continuity rule will take a lot of time, either for piano practice or for solfege, targeted practice in this manner will yield greater results far more quickly than singing or playing the entire piece over and over again from beginning to end. Practice does not make perfect. Perfect practice makes perfect, meaning practicing using an effective method.

Got It, Forgot It

By breaking down music into segments, and oscillating between practicing different segments, students discover what they grasp and don't grasp quickly. Forgetting and relearning challenging material repeatedly becomes easier over time, and reinforces both the material and the brain's ability to learn and relearn more quickly. Over time, learning becomes jogging the memory.

This also means practicing solidly for an hour is usually less effective than multiple 15 - 30 minute sessions. From the brain's perspective, having a chance to forget and relearn multiple times is equivalent to having multiple practice sessions, as opposed to a single practice session. This gives the subconscious time to mull over what occurred, and students will be surprised that what was difficult or impossible to practice in a previous session may be easier in a later session, even within the same day.

Tackle the Hardest First

When evaluating a new piece of music for the first time, break down the basics to immediately process how the piece starts, then rapidly scan the rest of the piece for challenging areas. At Juilliard, performers may have a few minutes to try out challenging areas, before doing a first official read. This is taking the concept of reading ahead a little further.

Mental Play

Mental play generally means running through music in your head, without using an instrument or your voice.

Not only is this useful, for example, in a subway system where no one will realize you are practicing solfege or a song you would like to sing, this is an essential skill to develop. Together with absolute pitch and sightreading skills, those adept at mental play know how a new piece of music will sound, and can immediately focus on challenging areas, even shaping the musicality, without singing a single note or touching a keyboard.

Anyone who is a vocalist must become adept at mental play, and this is why solfege training is so effective. Pianists can simply plunk a piano key without thinking about the note or having absolute pitch. Violinists need to do a little more work, because they will need to play a tuned note proficiently, and tune their playing with respect to the ensemble or orchestra. Vocalists, on the other hand, must generate their music 100%, without aid from any instrument. This requires that they know what note they will sing before they sing it.

There can be many aspects to mental play besides just hearing a tune in your head (ideally with the correct pitches). Additional approaches may include:

- Running through the correct solfege syllables for each pitch.
- Visualizing the sheet music.

- Running through the music faster or slower than the normal tempo.

- Thinking through what will happen both before and after a performance.

- Thinking through the start and end of a piece, since beginnings and endings have the largest impact on audiences. This includes visualizing a clean, cold start, and a dramatic finale.

- Being able to run through just the right or left hand.

- Playing your piece on your leg, without benefit of audio or tactile feedback from a keyboard (mental play can be done in conjunction with other physical components).

- Running through just a challenging section. Can you start from the middle using the correct starting pitch?

- Visualizing fingers on the correct keys (granted, at French School we were taught early not to look at the keys, and to develop our proprioceptive understanding instead).

- Visualizing conducting time to ensure that the note durations are fully understood and correct.

- Thinking through the musicality of a piece:

    o The best way is with a story. Is this sad? Happy? What happened? What kinds of emotions do you as a performer hope to communicate to your audience? How will it be communicated? Soft?

> Loud? Slow? Fast? Sweetly? Brusquely?

> ○ Can you run through the physics of motion mentally? In other words, acceleration and deceleration together with crescendos and decrescendos. How would music communicate a couple waltzing? A roller coaster ride? Spinning top, bumblebee, music box, or juggler?

- Anticipating how you will handle flubs during a performance.

- Thinking through how you will adapt to different performing conditions.

All mental play in these various forms will serve to reinforce, validate, and deepen the understanding of music and level of memorization. Mental play before a performance keeps the brain occupied, which can help alleviate nervousness.

Adding to the Foundation

Students who master the foundational aspects of the French School solfege methodology will have all of the tools needed to study any music-related subject and any musical genre - as a performer or composer. And, solfege training as outlined in this book gives students the ability to discern which courses, books, instructors, and conservatories are effective.

Here are some additional topics to help bridge the transition from foundation to higher learning opportunities.

Church Modes

These are also called Gregorian modes:

Dorian, phrygian, lydian, mixolydian, aeolian, and ionian.

While much of western music uses familiar major or minor scales, the other scales sound different. A dorian (D or re) scale is created by starting with re and playing all of the white keys up to re. A phrygian (E or mi) scale is created by starting with mi and playing all of the white keys up to mi.

You can transpose them. First evaluate a basic mode, e.g. dorian starting with re, and determine where the whole steps (w) and half steps (h) are between each of the notes.

    re mi fa sol la si do re

    w h w w w h w

To create a dorian scale starting with fa, replicate the pattern of whole and half steps for dorian, but starting with fa instead of re.

    w h w w w h w

    fa sol la♭ si♭ do re mi♭ fa

Even though these scales may be different, the accidentals still follow the rules:

    fa do sol re la mi si

    si mi la re sol do fa

Notice in F dorian the flats are still si♭ mi♭ la♭

Music that sounds Celtic tends to be in dorian, and music that sounds pastoral could very well be lydian.

Meter Lesson

Understanding straight time vs. compound time can be a challenge. French School alumnus Robert Taub once hosted a Juilliard doctoral forum about Beethoven's composition sketchbooks, noting even Beethoven sometimes started a sketch with straight time and later switched to compound time, or vice versa.

For time signatures, e.g. 4/4 or 6/8, the top number indicates the number of beats per measure (using these examples, 4 or 6), and the bottom number refers to the type of note that has one beat (here, a quarter note or eighth note).

For straight time, the top number could be 2, 4, 5, 7 and the bottom number will be 4. Metronome markings for straight time will be quarter note = tempo (half note or different duration if the tempo ends up being too slow or fast). General rule of thumb: tempos range between 50 and 200. Anything slower than 50 is slower than a human heartbeat, making this difficult to track accurately.

The important elements to consider for both straight and compound time are: *beat, division* (primary breakdown), and *subdivision*.

For straight time:

> *Beat:* quarter note
>
> *Division:* 2, so eighth notes

Subdivision: 2, so sixteenth notes

For compound time, the top number could be 6, 9, 12, 15 - some division of 3.

Beat: dotted quarter note

Division: 3, so 3 eighth notes

Subdivision: 2, so (2 16th, 2 16th, 2 16th)

When do you use straight time vs. compound time? Music that is in 3/4 time could also be written in 6/8 time. Here are some guidelines:

1. If a new composition in straight time has a lot of triplets, this is an indication to convert to compound time - e.g. from 4/4 to 12/8. 3/4 may become 9/8.

This is also part of a larger principle - the principle of least ink used. This tends to clean up sheet music, which is helpful to performers. Carillon Fantasies, a Juilliard exercise, is a good example of switching from straight to compound time (otherwise beyond the double bars, a lot of triplets would pop up). In this case, the tempo did change, but you can see the transition from quarter note = tempo to dotted quarter note = tempo.

* * *

Carillon Fantasies

*"I wish I may, I wish I might
Have this wish I wish tonight."*

Eileen Sauer

2. To switch between straight time and compound time signatures where the tempo remains the same, notate the change from compound to straight time using dotted quarter = quarter note or vice versa.

3. A musical work can be written in 4/4 or 8/8 depending on what the music does. Use 4/4 straight time if the feel of the beat is 1 and 2 and 3 and 4 and. Use 8/8 if the feel is more 123 123 12 (or 123 456 78 123 456 78).

5/4 and 10/8 work in a similar way. If the beat is 1 and 2 and 3 and 4 and 5 and, use 5/4. If the beat feels more like 123 123 1234, use 10/8.

One last brainteaser. What is 6/4? Is this straight or compound time?

Answer: This is still compound time because the top number is divisible by 3. However, because the denominator is 4 instead of

8, the beat is now a dotted half note, as opposed to a dotted quarter note. Added exercise: determine how the division and subdivision would break down for 6/4.

Beaming Notes

Always show the beat (at minimum, the first and third beats for a 4/4 bar, or the midpoint of each bar). This makes the music easier for performers to read, whether they are pianists or instrumentalists in an orchestra.

This is especially true when using professional music notation software like Sibelius, while composing works in unusual time signatures like 5/4. These tools don't always beam the notes correctly. You can also beam over rests, like in another part of Carillon Fantasies below. For pianists, this makes it easier to see how the left and right hands coordinate. For orchestras, this allows the conductor to easily see how the different instruments will work together.

Lead Sheets

Lead sheets are different from Western classical music notation in that they specify only the essential elements of a song. They can contain a melody line, lyrics, and chord symbols. Fake books contain a collection of lead sheets.

Coming from a classical piano background, I thought lead sheets were a watered down system of musical notation so that non-musicians who couldn't read sheet music well could still learn to play popular tunes. Boy was I wrong.

Famous classical music not only has everything notated by the composer in terms of all of the notes and dynamics, it has a history of performances that lead to standardized expectations for how the music should be performed.

When only the essence that defines a song is specified, this leaves performers with many different options. Do we:

- use chords? Broken chords?

- use a sequence of notes? A different sequence of those notes?

- syncopate the rhythms?

- play the song in this key, or transpose it?

In other words, lead sheets are a great way to study music theory, improvisation on the fly, and arranging music. Specifying the essence of a popular tune means the music will still be recognizable by the audience, and yet the performer can make each rendition uniquely their own interpretation.

Lead sheets are prevalent among instrumentalists, vocalists, and in some genres of music like jazz.

ABRSM

ABRSM stands for the Associated Board of Royal Schools of Music. This is an organization that has a national certification system to gauge where music students are in their progress. They can test proficiency in instruments, music theory, singing, jazz, etc. This started in England in the 1890s and is now available in 93 countries.

Using Solfege as a Tool

Once solfege students master the fundamentals to a point where nothing stops them, the possibilities become endless. They can learn an instrument, study music theory, and use solfege as a tool to learn about improvisation and composition. Granted, people have different strengths and weaknesses - for example - those who have a good ear may find themselves relying on that a lot and slowly and painstakingly writing down the sheet music for their latest composition. That's fine, as long as all of the fundamentals together give them enough information to bring their sheet music to an audition at a music conservatory.

What will often happen at that audition is that the interviewers may say things like: why did you write this in 5/4? This should be 10/8. Or yes, this is 6/4 but the notes in this bar are beamed incorrectly, and you've used the incorrect enharmonic equivalent here.

That's perfectly fine, as long as students have the basic ability to write sheet music that accurately reflects what is going on in their heads. Because then and only then can they begin to embark on a useful discussion with professors who can see exactly where they are, and help them.

Those who master solfege can sing in a choir, and be paid by a choir to help others who can't sightread as well but can pick things up by ear and memorize. They can arrange music for a quartet or band.

So how can solfege be used as a tool?

First, learn the fundamentals of how music works. The solfege methodology enables this.

Learn an instrument, and if that instrument is not piano, at least develop basic keyboard competency with the piano. Instrument ability will usually dictate the level to which a composer can aspire.

Read *The Study of Counterpoint* from Johann Joseph Fux's *Gradus ad Parnassum*, first published in 1725 and translated into English by Alfred Mann in 1965. I did things the hard way, meaning I simply went by what "sounded good" and what didn't. That's awfully vague and it took me decades to get to where I am today. Fux's work was studied by Haydn, Mozart, Beethoven, Liszt, etc. He begins with what intervals are consonant versus dissonant, and describes how music moves. With a few starting rules (analogous to training wheels on a bike), you won't be able to help yourself, you will begin composing and experimenting. Long before we knew about using the **S.M.A.R.T.** acronym (**S**pecific, **M**easurable, **A**chievable, **R**elevant, **T**ime bound) to fashion measurable, actionable goals, Fux did exactly that with *Gradus ad Parnassum*. This information became a solfege assignment one week, and students were jumping up and down and screeching because they immediately got it. By week two they were composing.

Improvisation

Introducing a young solfege student to improvisation on the piano can be fairly simple. Improvisation is first and foremost about learning patterns.

1. Start with the Twinkle Twinkle melody only. Then add a left hand accompaniment using three note chords like (do mi sol) and (do fa la).

2. Show how some chords in the end of Twinkle Twinkle seem related - (si fa sol) (sol si fa) (sol re fa) - like cousins or siblings. And they can be substituted in to give the song more variability or make it slightly different each time you play. Students can learn about concepts like inversion in a more advanced solfege class or music theory class.

3. Transition to repeated broken chord patterns: (do mi) sol or do (mi sol)

4. Then the do sol mi sol pattern.

5. Then the do mi sol mi do pattern.

6. Switch from 4/4 to 3/4 time and turn it into a waltz, adding little ornaments to the melody.

7. Here's the "I dropped my ice cream cone" pattern. Make it minor, sounding a little sad.

8. Transition back to a happy French-style march because I

bought myself another ice cream cone.

9. Get serious and throw in a little Bach-like left hand wandering around.

10. Add little Mozart ornaments ending with a typical Mozart flourish and little trills (granted, Mozart actually did a set of variations for Twinkle Twinkle).

Now, start with the Happy Birthday melody, and guess what?

Three note chords. Broken chords. Do sol mi sol pattern, etc up to Mozart.

Basic improvisation involves applying patterns to different melodies. In addition, performers need to develop the muscle memory to transition to different key signatures and transpose these different songs and patterns.

On the jazz side, there are patterns like Boogie Woogie, blues, Joplin ragtime, and standards like Ain't Misbehavin', Georgia On My Mind, etc.

From there, keep building a database of patterns - both classical and jazz - in increasing complexity. Cross over patterns, as an example, starting with serious Bach and blending into a warm and rich jazz landing.

This is the additional fifth prong to solfege, and ideally every student should be able to riff Twinkle Twinkle at least 20 different ways, whether they are studying classical, jazz, or both. This is the core foundation that leads to being able to play at a piano bar for a few hours in the evening, entertaining friends, family and customers, taking ad-hoc requests for favorite songs and riffing on them. How might Beethoven do Itsy Bitsy Spider? What would Debussy have done with the "A" Train?

Beginning improvisers can improvise up to a certain level of complexity and then they start to stumble or go a lot slower. This is because being a really good improvisor entails knowing all of the scales, arpeggios and finger exercises down cold in different keys. This requires a lot of drilling, to be able to improvise at full speed on the fly and transition from one key to another. While endless mindless hours of Hanon exercises are not a productive use of piano practice time, those who want to learn to improvise will need targeted, mindful practice to build a solid database of patterns that they can play in all keys, and can transition easily from one key to another because it is imbued in their muscle memory.

The key to understanding "improv" is that it's "practiced improv", based on building a core set of fundamentals. Having said that, what is detailed in my dad's piano practice book, and this solfege guide, can all work together to facilitate building this core database of patterns.

Composition

What is your relationship to music? Are you a listener? Performer? Composer?

Listeners can appreciate many things about music and develop preferences, even if they are not performers or composers.

Performers can appreciate music as listeners, can also appreciate that something is easy or difficult to play, and can appreciate all of the intricacies associated with learning the music from the perspectives of technique and musicality.

For those who embark on a journey to become composers, famous composers now become teachers. Are you trying to write a violin solo for a composition class when you've never played the violin? You might begin to ask:

> What is the range of a violin?
>
> What kinds of things can a violin play? Can it do arpeggios, can it handle large leaps?

A listener might appreciate a Beethoven violin concerto. A violinist understands the intricacies involved with performing that Beethoven concerto. The composer writing a violin solo for the first time, having never played the violin, might hear Beethoven laughing gleefully.

> "Finally! You begin to ask the right questions. Range, you ask? How about this?
>
> What kinds of patterns can the solo violinist play? How about that?"

And so on. Being a listener, performer, *and* composer is the best way to develop a mindset for asking questions others might not normally ask, and gain a deep understanding of music from the greatest composers (there are all sorts of secrets in composers' scores).

What kinds of techniques facilitate learning to compose?

One TED talk with Jennifer Lin and Goldie Hawn shows Goldie randomly choosing notes and Jennifer improvising something on the fly. Try doing the same thing, even daily, to improve composing skills. Study different styles, randomly pick notes, and try to compose in that style. Progress by:

- varying time signatures.

- using chords, and sequences of notes.

- picking just white notes randomly.

- adding the entire chromatic scale later.

Sight Singing Improvisations to Music

This is another way to improve composing skills in a more intentional way. Start singing with the radio using solfege skills, first by sight singing the melody, then harmonizing in thirds.

Huge leap: try harmonizing something completely different without ever singing the same note as the melody. Expect to sound like a train wreck for an entire month, but doing this on a regular basis will improve the ability to improvise on the fly.

Last: try harmonizing to music you've never heard. This is possible (musicians, especially jazz musicians, will often come together and create informal jam sessions) because those who practice long enough begin to understand the general structure of music and realize it's like crossing a river. If you try to cross the entire river you won't get there, but if you realize there are three possible options (stepping stones) in front of you, then you can hop on one of them and continue hopping down the trail until you realize there are three more options. Choose one, and continue until you have to make another choice. Eventually you get to the other side.

If you're not sure where the music is going, add a rest instead of a note for the first beat. As soon as you hear the first note or chord, you immediately know where the music is heading (your choices are visible again) and you can choose your stepping stone and continue hopping from stone to stone.

If you guess wrong, going off kilter is perfectly fine if it resolves later in that bar, or further down the line once you grasp where the music is really going.

Back to the flash card system of randomly choosing notes, I use this in two ways: to spark ideas for a composition, or to jog myself out of a creative block. I generally need at most three flash card draws to break out of a creative block. This is how effective the flash card technique can be.

More deliberate composing sessions:

- When starting out, you won't have good control. Explore

different chords, sequences, chord progressions.

- You usually have no coherence and will jump from one thing to another. Melodies will be short and wander initially.

While earlier works may be less refined, sometimes they're a much more honest window into a composer's psyche, because inexperienced composers lack the control to both compose and filter/polish their work simultaneously. Later it gets easier and more polished, but maybe also more mainstream. This is both good and bad.

The goal is to experiment and begin building your own database of patterns, of harmonies, progressions, and transitions that you like that make sense, things that you can begin to string together. As time passes, work to make those patterns longer and less repetitive.

Random Tips and Tricks

Don't end a day of composing by sticking a temporary bandaid on a composition. It's difficult to erase a bandaid ending. Leave it as ambiguous as possible, maybe it's an up or down sequence that can lead to many different options. Then sleep on it, or take a long walk and it will usually resolve itself. One theory is that ear worms occur if we hear part of something, and it will continue to loop and jangle in our brain until we mentally play the ending. If this is true, this explains a lot. If you're composing and stop in the middle, this is probably like creating an ear worm for your subconscious to work on.

Stencil composing: While its roots may have started in comedy, this is actually a serious technique. Instead of repeating the same pattern of notes over and over again, pretend you drew that pattern of notes using a stencil, take that stencil and move it up a fifth, down a third, etc.

Music progresses from start to finish and people may assume that's how it's composed, but many times composers may want to go back to the beginning or to some expansion of what was played at the beginning, or maybe they wrote the ending first. Learning to compose something that joins up with the original melody or some future melody is a good thing to practice.

When I first started composing, I had a bunch of cassette tapes with nothing but endless wandering around as I tried to compose something. Fast forward decades later, and I no longer worry about losing something. True, this has bitten me two or three times over these decades, but if I forget an idea, one of three things will happen. If it's worth keeping, it will resurface. Capture it in sheet music form. If it's not worth it, it won't reappear. If it's a half-baked germ of an idea, it tends to resurface later in a more mature form.

Fusion is another great sparker for creativity. Punk Bach or Punk Polka. Beethoven done in Ragtime. The possibilities are endless.

How can composers avoid stagnation? One solution is to do what the Philip Glasses of this world do. Play with every conceivable musician under the sun. Each new musician can introduce a whole new world of notes, rhythms, culture, etc. And this infuses into and expands the database of patterns.

Having a story in mind may facilitate creativity.

Deus ex machina refers to a plot device where a seemingly unsolvable problem is suddenly and abruptly solved with a contrived and unexpected intervention or some new event. The same thing can happen in music, especially with inexperienced composers who paint themselves into a corner. Learn to recognize this, how it is the crutch that it is, and eliminate it by learning how to make smooth, coherent transitions that make sense.

Improve your piano or instrument skills. Instrument skills, more than anything, will inform the level of technicality and musicality at which a composer can compose.

Having said that, performers never have enough time to practice and rehearse. Pushing the edges of the envelope and keeping compositions playable requires careful balancing. If performers can't devote a reasonable amount of practice time and play your compositions, how will you build communitas with performers and fans?

Compile a database of ideas. They may be the germ of ideas, unfinished compositions, snippets of music that ultimately did not fit into a completed work. One of those ideas may be the perfect launching point in a crunch when a composition assignment is due or a deadline is fast approaching.

Composition at Juilliard

A good composition professor has the ability to give technically precise enough information, without imposing any particular viewpoint. Composition classes in a conservatory offer an expanded world in learning to write for other instruments. Hearing Juilliard performers run through a 20 minute reading is illuminating in terms of learning what kind of music works for different instruments.

Students learn to notate music properly for performers and conductors, so there is no time wasted during a rehearsal or practice session. Different instruments have unique notations; for more information, the Samuel Adler orchestration book is a good reference.

Music can seem highly subjective, so how do you teach and critique about music? Have every student in the class refer to a specific measure or measures and provide one positive and one constructive comment.

The comments need to be precise and not fuzzy opinions or judgments (use the **S.M.A.R.T.** acronym to craft feedback that is **S**pecific, **M**easurable, **A**chievable, **R**ealistic, and **T**ime bound). Our professor will often ask questions and help us rephrase our feedback. After we are done, our professor will give his positive and constructive comments, often both agreeing and disagreeing with other students. This is invaluable. Instead of worrying about whether someone giving feedback is biased, soak in the totality of everyone's feedback, and choose which to consider.

Because each instrument has different characteristics and timbre, this can help composers to remain creative since the different characteristics will influence what composers write.

Constraints are another fun way to shake things up. Pick your favorite jazz chord structure and compose an entire piece around it (e.g. The Tarpit Dance).

What if you have a commission from a school band with very young, inexperienced members, so that you can only use quarter notes and longer duration, and a limited range in pitch?

What if the pianist can only perform with the left hand? Google Paul Wittgenstein.

Try writing a piano piece where the left and right hands play in different keys (Sibelius allows composers to choose different key signatures).

Music Notation Software

In solfege, students learn to deconstruct music that they hear and write it down in their dictation books. Once they've learned to do this proficiently, they may want to explore free music notation software like MuseScore. Notation software is useful both for creating printable music scores as well as playing those musical scores. Prior to studying at Juilliard, I used MuseScore and this served me well enough in a non-conservatory environment.

Once students land in a conservatory environment studying music composition or orchestration, they will likely discover their professors will mandate students use professional music notation software such as Sibelius, Finale, or Dorico (next generation Sibelius, created by the same development team that created Sibelius). The software is fairly expensive with a rich set of features and WYSIWYG ("what you see is what you get") capabilities for laying out a score exactly as you want it to appear. This is appropriate for those who are in a conservatory environment or truly serious about wanting professional scores and possibly instrument parts for ensembles or orchestras.

After three semesters taking music composition classes in the Evening Division at Juilliard, I compiled a checklist that my professor found useful. Feel free to download the PDF, and I've also included the checklist here. One item requires some explanation, and violin will serve as an example. Violinists understand slurs in music to indicate that notes should be played legato with one bow stroke. So the question is: how do violinists know the difference between slurred notes and tied notes? Our composition professor discouraged the use of slurs over repeated notes, because it can be difficult to distinguish between tied notes and repeated notes with a slur over them.

What is listed in this checklist is specific to Sibelius. If anyone else uses Finale, feel free to create an addendum for Finale users. This checklist is not meant to be comprehensive, but lists critiques that arise consistently in our composition classes. As of December 2017, the assessment from Juilliard classmates is that Dorico will have a full-featured release soon.

Sibelius Notation Checklist

Basics - Score (including Juilliard-specific)

☐ Tempo markings in correct bold font (Text > Styles > metronome mark)

☐ Ideal: stick to metronome values (Google metronome wiki for values, e.g 126 vs 123)

☐ Wide enough margins so performers can write notes

☐ Each staff system doesn't have too many bars (in general 1 - 2 less bars than Sibelius default)

☐ Enough space between each staff (in general 1 line less than Sibelius default)

☐ Title, composer name, exercise number on each page, page numbers on pages 2 on

☐ Appearance > Accidentals and Dots - Uncheck "Restate accidental when note is tied across a system break"

☐ Layout > Document Setup - Set page size to Concert (9 x 12") and (for piano) change staff size from default 0.28 to 0.24. This looks more like published music, and allows for more notes on a page

---

☐ Instruments in correct order (in general use orchestral order?) More on parts later

☐ First line of music has correct instrument names? e.g. Violin I, Violoncello

☐ Subsequent lines of music have correct abbreviated instrument names?

☐ Measure numbers at the start of each line, large enough?

☐ If accidentals are crowded, use (Sibelius) Appearance > Note Spacing

☐ Correct fonts? If too small or not bolded performers may not see. (use Text > Styles to get right format and placement)

☐ `<ctrl e>` for expression markings, highlight l (ell) for line markings like **rit** and **accel**

☐ Oddball last line? Use page breaks or system breaks to create a last line with a few bars

Basics - Music

☐ Correct key signature (or no key signature if chromatic)?

☐ No more than 4 sharps or flats in key signature? If so, re-key (e.g. from D# to D) or set to no / atonal key signature

☐ Pickup bar must only include beats with notes, e.g. 4th beat pickup will show one quarter note, not dotted half rest and quarter note

☐ Don't start piece with a fermata

☐ Correct meter? (e.g. straight or compound time?) If lots of triplets, consider converting to compound time, or vice versa

☐ Correct marking for tempo changes with respect to meter, e.g. straight time quarter note = x, compound time dotted quarter = x

☐ Correct marking if no tempo changes? e.g. quarter = dotted quarter, or dotted quarter = quarter, etc.

☐ Tempo range between 50 and 200? e.g. change from quarter = 200 to half = 100

☐ Double barline to denote all key and time signature changes

---

☐ Correct clef for each instrument? e.g. viola is in tenor clef

☐ If strange time signatures (e.g. 5, syncopated times) do notes need to be re-beamed and tied to show beats?

☐ Beam over rests to show beats?

☐ For time signatures like 7/4 or 13/8, consider breaking down, e.g. alternating 3/4 and 4/4

☐ Enharmonically correct? If a mix of sharps and flats, see if changing some will clean up the score

☐ Cautionary accidentals? Especially if sharp in one hand and natural in the other hand (piano)

☐ Where can the principle of "least amount of ink used" be applied? e.g. change quarter rest eighth rest to dotted quarter rest (while still obeying the "show beat" rule)

☐ Avoid ending with 16th rest, e.g. turn 16th note 16th rest into 8th note

---

☐ Not too many tempo changes (unless this is a conductor challenge)? Each tempo change results in a minute lost during a 20 minute reading

☐ Final tempo marked at the end of every **rit** or **accel**?

☐ If there is a fermata, fermata must show in all parts, on the same beat in all parts (e.g. break up rests if necessary)

Dynamics

☐ In general, don't start with *mp*, use *mf* or *p* or *f*

☐ Are dynamic markings in the right place? e.g. expression markings / hairpins etc below music (in the middle for piano), tempo / **rit** / **accel** / pizz etc above the music. If not, performers won't see them.

☐ If creating multiple voices, use voices 1 and 3 they will line up perfectly. With voices 1 and 2 you'll have to mess with the score to line things up

☐ Sibelius can split key signatures in score, e.g. violin in G and viola in D

Strings

☐ Bow markings (or mark legato)

☐ Correct markings for arco, pizz, legato, etc.

☐ Make sure enough time to switch from arco to pizz, etc.

☐ Glissando marked from notehead to notehead?

☐ Valid double and triple stops?

☐ Short, choppy passages go against the strengths of using stringed instruments

☐ Sibelius may not show glissando if crowded, create less measures per line

☐ Double bass notated one octave higher

☐ Double bass is slower speaking instrument, bass has more opening on start, don't write fast. Everyone else can play fast

Piano

☐ If pianist is amenable, deliver fully notated PDF score beforehand, and MIDI playback as well

☐ In general avoid adding pedal markings (or notate "pedal freely"), leave up to performer

☐ Change clef if too many ledger lines

☐ Test to make sure notes work with hand positioning (especially cross over)

Winds

☐ Clarinet score notated in B♭? Marked on the score as notated in B♭?

☐ Keep track of what happens with key signature when you transpose - get fa# do#. Sibelius - no key option

☐ Clarinet low notes are warm and soft, high notes are loud and piercing. Not possible to do high notes pianissimo

☐ Note: You Can write long passages, if you know that the clarinetists can circular breathe

☐ Legato - need slur, otherwise they will tongue the individual notes

Conducting

☐ No GP (general pause) during a page turn (it's noisy during the silence)

☐ If there is a GP, also put a fermata so that the conductor isn't forced to conduct time during the GP

Vocal

☐ Avoid really weird intervals, keep as diatonic as possible. Other instruments are easier to play, or you may have to tune (e.g. strings). Singer has to generate sound from scratch

☐ High notes? Create an ossia, the singer will treat this as a challenge

☐ Dynamic markings above the staff for singers because lyrics are below

---

☐ Lyrical extension lines (extend to tied notes)

☐ Comma in lyrics comes before extension line

☐ Sibelius won't always show extension lines, may need to have less measures per line

---

☐ Tenor - treble clef but small 8 - written an octave down

☐ All female voices written at clef

☐ Singers never change clef

☐ Possible to write outside normal range if you write for a particular singer, e.g. sopranos can sing lower (belting)

☐ Voice tends to get richer and darker with age

☐ Range from low - belting, weak area, golden area (can sing strong and loud), up to high

☐ Keep high notes as climax, and sparse, don't burn out singer

☐ High notes: consonants much harder to vocalize

☐ High notes nothing less than f dynamic

Instrumental Parts

☐ Each instrument part clearly notated at beginning of part score with instrument name in large font? e.g. Violin I

☐ Correct format depending on context? Parts for string quartet, piano with voice - piano has the full score

☐ Large enough for performer to read from afar (e.g. while holding a violin)?

☐ Collisions eliminated (e.g. double slurs, cue names above note, rehearsal marks)

☐ Correct clef for instrument? (Cues may mess up clef.)

☐ Clef for viola depends on ledger lines and what they can comfortably read. Violinist may not be able to read tenor clef. If lots of ledger lines, re-clef. Clef changes should a minimum of 2 bars, avoid lots of clef changes.

☐ Enough cues (or small staves) for performer? (you can never have too many)

☐ Cues all stem up?

☐ Cues in correct clef?

☐ Cues correctly transposed? (e.g. If horn part, flute cue needs to be transposed)

☐ If intricate interplay between instruments, consider cue staff (small staff with blank lines hidden)

☐ Parts printed single side, not stapled or bound so performers can do what they want (e.g. tape them accordion style)

☐ Does music account for page turns?

☐ Parts marked solo or tutti where appropriate?

☐ Are you using a fermata where the fixed number of beats would be better? e.g. fermata or GP followed by everyone trying to synchronize is hard

☐ Analyze performer markings on parts after class

Reading

☐ First to arrive are first to be performed. Place parts on correct stand behind and underneath parts that are already there (pros/cons: first reading may be warm up, players fresh. Later readings they may be tired)

☐ Do the performers bounce around to look at other parts? May indicate a need for more cues, etc.

☐ Pianist: can have double sided in 3 ring binder, make sure music accounts for page turns. If single pages or page turns are a challenge (music dense, or pianist cannot read ahead enough), can lay out 2 or 3 and page turner can overlay on top. Future (and present options): iPad with foot pedal to turn pages

Advanced Students

In our solfege classes, not only do we ask questions to see if students grasp basic concepts related to time signatures, note pitches, durations, and key signatures, we ask questions to see if they understand what the right questions are to ask, and why. The goal is for students to develop deep knowledge by learning how to deconstruct new music on their own, as well as mentor other students.

Coaching Leaders

Teach the class to ask the right questions.

When looking at a new assignment, ask the class: "what is the first question that I ask?". The response from the more advanced students will be: "what is the time signature?" This sets the stage immediately for beginner students to start thinking at a meta level.

Also ask questions like: what is the first note, what type of note/rest is this (duration like half note).

- What are the sharps and flats?
- Given these two sharps, what key is this in?
- Is this major or minor? Etc.

Ask them what other questions should we ask?

Enlist advanced students as teaching assistants.

At French School, advanced students play the role of teaching assistant by asking 2 or 3 questions for a new assignment, and determining whether the beginner group gives correct answers. If a beginner is one note off, coach the advanced student to say "close!"

Coach the advanced students to monitor beginners and ensure they keep their eyes on the music and follow along.

During dictation (simple exercise first for the beginners), have one advanced student up at the chalkboard, writing clefs, time signatures, key signatures, and notes if necessary. Have other advanced students monitor the progress of the beginner students, validate their work, and indicate when they have finished so the instructor can continue.

Forcing students to think at a meta level will also expedite learning an instrument. They will begin to think automatically the way all great musicians think, so that their teachers can focus on technique and musicality. Given that modern musicians rarely have enough time to practice, the efficiencies laid out in my dad's piano practice guide and this solfege guide are not a luxury, but a necessity in order to be a good musician. We attended a Game of Thrones live concert experience at Madison Square Garden, and learned from the composer that he has two weeks to put together the music for each episode. And that is a luxury, normally he has one week.

Pair beginning and advanced students.

Drill by having an advanced student and beginner student go to the blackboard. Have the advanced student say a solfege note, and low or high if necessary, and the beginner student has to write that note. The advanced student says whether the answer is correct or not.

Teach students how to divide and conquer.

What we do in solfege is a metaphor for life itself. Big problems are often just a number of little problems masquerading as big problems. A big problem often isn't a tiger that is going to eat you, it is really composed of a bunch of kittens that need your help.

What is the big problem that we are trying to solve?

"Can you pick up a piece of music you've never seen or heard before and figure it out?"

What are the little problems that help us to solve this big problem?

- What is the time signature?
- What is the top number and what does it mean?
- What is the bottom number and what does it mean?
- Is this treble or bass clef?
- How many sharps or flats are there?
- What key is this in?
- Is this major or minor?
- Do we start on the first beat? If not, what beat?

Teach students to think cross-functionally.

We often treat subjects in school in a siloed manner, where we think we are learning music, math, science, and English. These subjects are often intertwined. In solfege, we are using our math skills.

For example: If we have a time signature of 4/4, and turn each quarter note into a triplet, how many triplets will be in this measure?

4 x 3 = 12: 1 and and 2 and and 3 and and 4 and and

or

1 2 3   4 5 6   7 8 9   10 11 12

Advanced Exercises

Chose a random easy exercise from Dannhäuser book 1 which is likely in do major. Have students transpose and solfege this in another key on the fly. First ask them to determine how many sharps / flats the key would have, and what they are. Yes, this means the accompanist has to transpose on the fly as well... This is great practice for improvisation drills. Also, start with keys that only have one sharp or flat. Then two, etc.

Chose a random exercise, and have the accompanist play the exercise with the melody. Have students sight sing an improvised secondary voice. Initially, sight sing in thirds, either above or below the melody line. Once they reach a level of proficiency, have them improvise a secondary voice without singing the same note as the melody.

Ear training: prior to repeating the notes played by the teacher, have students call out the solfege notes that were played before playing them on the second piano. This will reinforce solfege mental play.

Performance Preparation

Many solfege students also take instrument lessons and perform, so these previously published blog posts are included.

History

Saturday afternoon on 4/30/2016, there was a benefit concert for The French School of Music. I sat on a bench with the other performers, next to a French School alumnus, waiting to play. What unfolded during the concert had me flashing back to an experience in 1973, so I'll start there first.

In 1973, during my first MEC (Music Education Council) NJ State piano competition, I was waiting in line with other competitors in my age group to perform (I was eight at the time). I looked to my left and saw a boy slouched back in his chair, his arms wrapped around his stomach. He looked pale and upset. I asked him if he was OK, and he groaned: "no. I don't want to go up there and play, I have butterflies in my tummy!" Well *thanks*. Once I learned he had butterflies in his tummy, I had butterflies in my tummy.

He went up and played before me, since we were playing in age order (oldest to youngest) from left to right. He wasn't a student at my piano school so he played differently than my piano teacher had coached me, but he did OK and walked off. Then it was my turn. After I was done, my mom and piano teacher wanted to know what the heck had happened. They said I was so nervous everyone could see it, and my left leg was shaking badly while I was on stage. My poor teacher had trained me well but she didn't anticipate being blindsided by a non-French School competitor who had accidentally (?) stumbled on the perfect method for derailing a fellow competitor. That year, the student with butterflies in his tummy came in first place, and I came in third. The next year, I came in first place and he came in fifth.

But the performance anxiety never left me, and most times I performed at around 80% of what I was capable of doing when I was playing privately without an audience. While I played at Carnegie Recital Hall nine times as a child, most of those were as a second place winner. It wasn't until years later when, as a software developer branching into technical training, I thought about my past experiences as a pianist, and decided it was silly for me to suffer from stage fright. By using my early music education and gaining consistent experience doing technical training, I got over my fears and taught well over 1000 people Sybase, Java, and object-oriented technology.

Fast forward to this benefit concert in 2016. The performer sitting next to me said: "I am so nervous!!" I'm thinking wait, you're in med school and you practice three hours a day, why are you nervous?! And given my experience in 1973, this wasn't helping me one darn bit. I hadn't performed musically in years, or consistently musically in decades, and I was supposed to end the performance program with a world premiere of my own composition. He bemoaned how, when performing another work, he completely blanked on how it started, and if he could get through the first four bars of his piece, he thought he'd be OK. This was a much younger alumnus and I used this rationale to gently persuade my fist of death not to try and land a solid punch.

I told him something I'd learned years ago, to try and help him reframe his perspective. What we may register as fear - e.g. increased, rapid heart rate - is our body's way of preparing us to be maximally effective when we need to perform. The heart is pumping more blood, which means more oxygen to the brain helping us stay alert, and more fuel to our muscles to move effectively. His face lit up and he appreciated that tip. It didn't fully stop him from continuing to voice his fears, and in spite of my knowing this little gem, my anxiety was starting to increase to a point where even these types of tips were not fully effective. But in retrospect I'm grateful this happened, because this led to concrete insights and methods for slaying this particularly nefarious dragon when it rears its ugly head. Here is what I added to the above gem that allowed me to short circuit a challenging situation.

I thought about the various breathing techniques in yoga classes, and settled on one where I closed my eyes and took a slow deep breath in through my nose as far as I could, then held it for five seconds. I then exhaled slowly through my mouth as far as I could exhale, holding it for five seconds. And then I kept repeating the process until my heart rate had slowed to a more manageable pace. This, together with the reframing technique, worked for me.

I'm glad this alumnus brought up the fears that he brought up. They can be addressed with the correct practice techniques and prior preparation.

The best way to address fear is to practice thoroughly before the concert. This, plus the two above techniques, maximize your chances of having a performance where you are able to play to the end without stopping. This means using the continuity rule, working on the hardest parts of the piece first, working on the beginning and ending first (since this is what audiences and judges remember the most), and having informal dry run performances prior to a competition.

To address fear of blanking when starting a piece, practice clean, cold starts regularly. Wake up, go to your keyboard, start your piece (or see if you can play straight through). Grab breakfast, then do another cold start. Before you leave the house, try another cold start. The goal is to be able to start playing your piece, cleanly and without stopping and restarting multiple times ("stuttering", which is a bad habit that disciplined cold start practice can eliminate).

If you're waiting to play and wondering if you can still remember how to play the first few bars, play them on your leg. This is another good technique to learn - how to practice without a keyboard that gives you audial and tactile feedback.

Because I have absolute pitch and pick up music quickly by ear, I've always done my performances by memory and that is another source of reinforcement. This particular alumnus started lessons at French School after solfege classes had stopped (this is difficult to do if there aren't enough students, and requires younger teachers able to keep up with often energetic, young students). As a result, while he was a performing beast, he hadn't had ear training and didn't always know all of the intervals, and while he heard music in his head, he didn't know enough to write it down. Our solfege classes at French School gave all students a consistent foundation in singing on pitch, sight singing, ear training, conducting time, and music dictation.

Conversely, performers who have excellent sightreading skills and a large repertoire may prefer using music during a performance. In this case, music can also serve as reassurance against blackouts.

The last tip I will discuss ended up being a challenge for me. Since our new solfege class was also singing at this concert, we had a rehearsal at the concert location (a church) the day before the concert. As a volume test I played part of my composition. The mistake I made was not running through the entire piece when I had a chance, and the piano had just been tuned and I thought everything was just fine.

The next day, I was puzzled when another French School alumnus mentioned the action was difficult to play, as the other performers had 2 hours prior to the concert to acclimate to the environment and grand piano. I played part of my composition again, at half speed, as we were taught to end at medium speed prior to our performance. This is a great way to prevent strange glitches from popping up just prior to your performance.

With all of these techniques I was as well prepared as I could be, but as I viewed the video afterwards I realized with the adrenaline I'd played at a pretty good pace, and nearly derailed at the tougher parts toward the end. That's because I have an electronic keyboard at home (due to urban space constraints) so I didn't have full endurance for a grand piano with a mellow upper half, and when I finally played the difficult parts at full speed, I realized this alumnus was right in saying the action was hard to play. It was fine for less technical and slower playing, but for those of us doing challenging works at full speed, the action wasn't quite up to snuff.

In cases like this, several things come to mind. If you are not a star performer who can request, for example, which Steinway grand you will rent for your upcoming performance, it would help to know your environment well prior to the concert. If it's early enough, it may even influence what kinds of pieces you choose to perform. If you learn during a dry run (or worse, during the performance) that the instrument isn't up to snuff, professional musicians know how to adapt on the fly - to breathe more frequently, slow down and add stylistic rubatos to navigate areas that become too challenging with an unregulated action. That happened with most of the performers at this concert.

Playing at the end can be a challenge, as this can increase the anxiety. Or, it may actually help. When other performers have trouble with the action, and they bemoan their missed notes and flubs, it's nice knowing you're all in the same boat and that can actually relieve some of the pressure. It did for me, and made me that much more aware when I had to adapt on the fly. As a result, while I had missed notes, I was able to start and get to the end of the piece without stopping.

I survived the very first world premiere of one of my compositions. And sometimes, that's all that counts.

Tips and Tricks

1. Tune your piano.

If you don't have absolute pitch, practicing on tuned instruments can help you develop absolute pitch. If you have absolute pitch, playing on out-of-tune instruments can cause you to lose your absolute pitch.

2. Try playing on different pianos periodically.

Visit a piano store or music school, for example. Maybe the lower half of one piano is out of tune. Another might not have been regulated in a decade. A third might have a more muffled upper half and brilliant lower half. Another has lovely bell tones in the higher octaves. This trains both your muscle memory and your brain to deal with different playing conditions and still be able to adapt and perform. You don't need to do this too often, just enough to get a feel for how you react and adapt. Don't practice for very long on an out of tune piano or you risk losing your sense of pitch.

3. Be careful about learning new material prior to performing.

Have you ever had this happen to you? You have a stable repertoire of pieces to perform. Then you try to learn something new and your muscle memory and repertoire suddenly destabilizes, you can't play it flawlessly anymore, and you have to work to re-stabilize it. This is normal. Once you understand this, you'll want to plan your piano practice carefully, making sure you can work on a stable repertoire prior to a performance.

Plan B: recognize that last minute changes prior to performing will require its own kind of practice so that you're not derailed.

Plan C: learn to adjust around hiccups during performances. Classes in improvisation have become more of a requirement, not just for a well-rounded education, but for getting around hiccups without visibly stopping, backing up, and restarting.

4. Repeatedly "get it", "forget it", "get it", "forget it"...

Give yourself enough prep time to be able to periodically stop practicing for a week or long enough to forget, and pick it up again. This may seem counterintuitive initially, but relearning reinforces deeper understanding, and makes you more aware of where the problem areas are (where you "forget").

5. Learn how to perform (separately from learning how to practice).

There are many tips and tricks to learn, think about, and rehearse so they become automatic the day of the performance. For example:

- What will you say if your piece has a description?

- When will you bow?

- When you sit, do your hands sit comfortably on the keyboard? Where are your elbows relative to the keyboard? Practice adjusting the piano bench to the correct height.

- Is the grand piano set up correctly (closed? Short stick? Long stick?)

- If this is a formal concert and you are wearing a long gown or tuxedo, do a dry run performance.
    - Is the gown so long that you walk awkwardly to get on and off stage? Do your heels catch in the hem?
    - Do your shoes have a hard bottom (do they click when you lift your foot and hit the pedal)? Are the soles rounded such that your foot slips off the pedal easily?
    - Do your long sleeves / jacket interfere with the keyboard?
    - Are your clothes so restrictive they hamper your full range of movement?

- Did you trim your nails so they don't get caught in the keys?

Know the environment in which you will perform. Ideally test your whole performance at full speed to test keyboard action. Adjust your playing and musical expressiveness if necessary.

If a group is performing:

- How will you file on and off the stage in an organized

manner?

- In what order will you enter and exit the stage? (If performers are different heights, what layout works aesthetically?)

- How far apart do the performers need to be? For example, if this is a solfege demo, is there enough space for performers to conduct time?

Maintain awareness to the very end of your performance, even (especially!) if you mess up. You are not done until both hands have left the keyboard. Don't daydream, go into autopilot, or think you're done prior to this. At one competition a student was upset with his performance. He simply stood up at the end of his piece with his hands still on the keyboard, and walked off stage quickly while looking down and shaking his head.

For public speaking engagements, some of the more valuable tips are not to look directly at the audience but above their heads (they won't be able to tell). Pan your gaze from left to right and front to back to give the entire audience a sense of personal engagement.

6. Record yourself, both audio and video.

You'll be surprised to learn what quirky habits you have, nervous or otherwise. Garageband is great because you can slow the tempo and analyze your playing in detail, and check the volume of individual notes.

7. Nip the yips.

In a television episode of Nip Tuck, Dr. Sean McNamara suddenly developed a "yip" - an involuntary uncontrollable movement, making it impossible for him to safely perform surgery, endangering his career. The same can happen to musicians. They'll be practicing as usual, and just prior to their performance they'll suddenly develop a strange "yip" and wonder where it came from and how to get rid of it.

The best way to prevent yips is to end your piano practice by playing half speed. My theories for why this works:

- You're less likely to make mistakes, and this leaves your subconscious with "homework" to do that involves correct play.

- Playing half speed is the equivalent of enunciating clearly, whereas if you played fast all the time, eventually you would begin to slur and lose the details.

- If you did encounter a yip at fast speed, practicing correctly at slow to half speed would retrain your fingers, and finishing at half speed would allow your subconscious to flush away the yip.

- Studies have shown that "ear worms" are caused by listening to part of a song, instead of the entire song. Taking a challenging part of your piece and playing it at half speed may be a way to use the "ear worm" trick to your advantage.

8. Even veteran performers who have never had problems may suddenly develop performance anxiety.

At one French School recital, a "veteran" who had performed flawlessly since toddlerhood blacked out during a recital (she might have been 14 at the time). Her world suddenly flipped, and things she'd never needed to pay attention to in the past now had her flummoxed. For a number of recitals after, she continued to have blackouts until she finally found her way out of the jungle, probably in a similar manner to what I had to do.

You never know when something may happen, and all of the sudden this information becomes relevant. Don't think because you're a seasoned veteran who has never screwed up, that you're immune.

9. Don't dwell on the negative.

Clearly, this is easier said than done. Someone could say "don't be nervous" and gee thanks, now you're nervous. The performer sitting next to you could be nervous, and that's not going to help you one darn bit.

This is why the tips like reframing your perspective and breathing techniques are important (previous section). These are concrete things you can do to keep yourself mentally, emotionally, and physically engaged to prevent / short circuit vicious spirals into fear and outright panic. Here is another tip: smelling a peeled orange and flowers will naturally calm you down. The human brain has a finite amount of bandwidth. If you are focusing on something else you cannot become or remain fearful. Consider these tips to be a start. Each person is different, and will need to find what works for them.

10. Control what you can within your environment.

If you get cold easily, bring a jacket. Temperatures in performance halls are often cold because during a packed performance, there are a lot of human batteries heating up the place. Consider carrying a set of gloves, hand lotion, handkerchief, etc.

I'm writing this last part after attending a 10-hour Chopin marathon in June 2016 with a number of different performers, at least 10 from Juilliard. After our experience with the benefit concert where we all seemed to have problems with the piano (I learned after our French School benefit concert one veteran was in tears after her performance), I wondered if the artists in the Chopin marathon ran into the same problem with their piano. Most had problems until one artist nailed her Chopin Fantasie, and then I realized it was possible to play on that piano. The performers seemed to do better as time passed, and I wonder if, like us, enough feedback had to get back to the other performers so they were aware and could figure out how to compensate. I was dying to walk up to the piano and test my theory but a. I didn't want to be the one all-day pass holder to get thrown out of the marathon midway and b. by the end of the marathon I was so wiped out I just wanted to go home. So we would need to hear from the performers to validate any of this. Seeing this many performers, it was interesting to note how each adapted differently to the environment. Some pulled it off and some didn't.

The other indications I had to support my theories: midway through there was an unscheduled delay to retune the piano (which isn't going to help if the issue is an unregulated piano, and even my husband noticed there was a strange resonance when the tuner played some of the lower notes). At one point the spokesperson mentioned how true professionals hide the pain, complexity and messiness of organizing these types events behind closed doors, showing only a calm, professional exterior. But you wouldn't believe what is going on behind closed doors right now, with all the behind-the-scenes activity… And I'm thinking: "aaayup. I bet I know exactly what's going on back there, especially if they know this piano is not regulated for optimal performance…"

"We had the piano tuned three days ago" isn't enough. The organizer has to give the tuner enough time to check if the piano needs to be regulated as well. An intermediate level pianist may not notice it but the Juilliard Ferrari gunning for Mach 10 will.

Curriculum

This is a proposed curriculum for music students to progress from beginner to advanced to beyond. This lists everything that is needed, from the perspective of the French School method, for students to become self-sufficient learners capable of stepping into a conservatory environment.

Depending on the student (and the teacher), a level could require anywhere from one to three years to achieve mastery. The curriculum isn't necessarily divided into even chunks of material designed to be accomplished in, for example, straight two year time periods. Rather, it is designed with certain cut-off points in mind that enable students to demonstrate they have reached another level of proficiency. Because students have varying capabilities, they will likely demonstrate proficiency at multiple levels for varying competencies.

This curriculum is designed for competencies regardless of how genetics may influence a student's capabilities, e.g. the ability to develop absolute pitch. While a number of French School alumni developed absolute pitch or were close, I know a few excellent pianists and piano teachers who are tone deaf.

To become self-sufficient musicians, students will want to strive to master the first three levels. Levels four and five are more specialized, for music students wanting to become composers or become self-sufficient pianists.

In addition to covering music-related topics and competencies, an additional goal is to help students learn how to learn, and how to navigate a world in which VUCA (an acronym that describes volatility, uncertainty, complexity, and ambiguity) accurately describes the general conditions and situations that are now the norm rather than the exception.

Level 1

Demonstrates basic competency in sight singing, ear training, conducting, music dictation.

- Understands the solfege pitches using the French method (do re mi fa sol la si).

- Understands durations of notes and rests including whole, half, eighth, sixteenth, triplet, dotted notes.

- Can successfully two-hand tap quarter note and quarter rest rhythms.

- Develops absolute pitch for middle do, re, and mi. Or, given a starting pitch, becomes indistinguishable from someone who has absolute pitch. Both groups can identify all notes in the do major scale and can successfully navigate two piano ear training.

- Can sing a base note (optionally played on a keyboard) and simple do major interval before playing the notes on a piano.

- Understands and can describe the basic process for breaking down new music.

- Demonstrates the ability to coach beginning students in learning how to break down new music.

Students can begin learning this from age five or younger, and some students may learn to read music before they learn to read the alphabet. Don't water down the curriculum, rather, expect that students age five or younger may take a year of slightly more rote learning before things begin to "click" from an awareness standpoint.

Level 2

- Knows how to read bass clef.

- Knows the sharps and flats and all key signatures.

- Understands the concept of chromatic solfege syllables (do, di, re, ri, etc.).

- Understands the concept of fixed do vs. movable do.

- Understands terms like tonic, dominant, diatonic, major, minor, relative minor, triad, inversion, etc.

- Understands the intervals (major, minor, augmented, diminished, tritone, etc.).

- Can successfully navigate ear training through all of the sharps and flats.

- Can successfully navigate two and three chord two piano ear training.

- Can successfully sing a root note (optionally played by the instructor) and notes of a triad or inversion before playing on a keyboard.

- Can transpose from one key to another.

- When singing up, then singing down, if the middle note is do, it remains do. It does not slip into do# or re.

- Able to successfully two-hand tap more complex patterns

including the duplet / triplet pattern.

Level 3

- Demonstrates basic proficiency with MuseScore (free music notation software) or Sibelius, Finale, or Dorico (if students have the money, time, desire or need to use professional music notation software).

- Understands alto and tenor clef and how to read the notes.

- Understands the church modes (e.g. dorian, phrygian, lydian).

- Transposes church modes (e.g. dorian in fa)

- Has read through *Study of Counterpoint*, from Johann Joseph Fux's *Gradus ad Parnassum*

- Understands lead sheets.

- Understands the difference between straight and compound time.

- Understands the importance of beaming music correctly, and always showing the beat.

- Demonstrates the ability to do completely random, atonal two piano ear training.

- Demonstrates the ability to sightread a solfege exercise from Dannhäuser Book 1, transpose mentally, then sing in another key.

Level 4

For music students wanting to become composers:

- Uses solfege as a tool to learn about composition and improvisation.

- Demonstrates various ways to compose: flash card method, stencil composing, harmonizing, and creating variations on a theme.

- Can compose given an assignment with specific parameters to follow.

- Can sight sing an improvised, secondary voice from a lead sheet, on pitch and using correct solfege notes.

- Uses music notation software to correctly notate own compositions.

- Composes solfege exercises for solfege class to sightread.

- Can compose and notate their own composition as a lead sheet.

Level 5

For music students interested in becoming self-sufficient pianists:

- Demonstrates ability to accompany solfege class.

- Demonstrates ability to adapt the accompaniment to students of different skills.

- Improvises from lead sheets.

- Can play a melody with left hand, conduct with right hand, and solfege.

- Can accompany a Level 3 student in singing a transposed Dannhäuser solfege exercise.

- Can take a composed exercise from a Level 4 student and improvise a piano accompaniment.

Exercises

When groups of students are singing their number, or students are doing ear training individually at the second piano, keep students sitting in their seats engaged with exercises they can write in their music dictation book. Since the class is usually varied, having exercises that start at the beginner level and progress to intermediate and advanced level will allow students to work at their own pace. Over time, more advanced students can start with the intermediate level or advanced level exercises. They can mentor beginners through the exercises if they have free time.

- Beginner exercises test students' knowledge of pitches and note durations.

- Intermediate exercises can test concepts related to sharps and flats, figuring out notes with ledger lines, key signatures, etc.

- Advanced exercises tend to run the gamut in terms of concepts discussed, and creativity of the exercises.

Sample 1

Everyone write the number, then the note in your dictation booklet:

1. re (whole note), 2. high mi (quarter note), 3. do (half note), 4. la (eighth note), 5. high do (dotted half note), 6. mi (dotted quarter note), 7. si (whole note), 8. fa (quarter note), 9. hi fa (half note), 10. sol (dotted quarter note)

If you finish, and this is correct, **intermediate** level using all quarter notes:

1. fa#, 2. si flat, 3. do#, 4. re flat, 5. la natural, 6. mi flat, 7. la sharp

Question: which pairs of notes will sound exactly the same, and why?

Advanced:

Listed are a base note, and an interval. Write the correct chord using quarter notes.

As an example:

do third is the chord (do mi)

1. re fifth, 2. mi third, 3. do fourth, 4. low si (octave), 5. fa fifth, 6. sol sixth, 7. la fourth 8. mi flat fifth, 9. do seventh, 10. do ninth

Sample 2

Everyone write the number, then the note:

1. la (whole note), 2. low si (quarter note), 3. middle do (half note), 4. hi re (eighth note), 5. mi (dotted half note), 6. si (dotted quarter note), 7. low la (whole note), 8. hi mi (quarter note), 9. re (half note), 10. hi fa (dotted quarter note)

If you finish, and this is correct, **intermediate** level:

1. Write the solfege notes for the sharps by memory

2. Given a key signature of one sharp, state the sharp, then state the rule to figure out the major key, and use whole notes to write out the major scale. Note: put the correct key signature

3. Given a key signature of two sharps, use whole notes to write out the major scale

Advanced: Writing bass clef - note what *middle do* is in treble and bass clef. If you're new to bass clef, you can start from middle do and work your way down the scale.

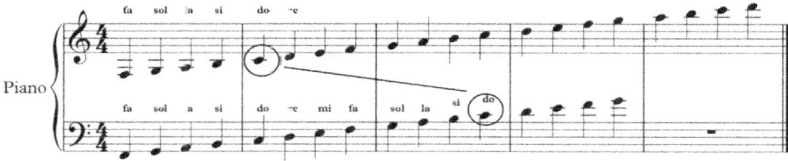

This is Mary Had a Little Lamb in both treble and bass clef, where bass clef is one octave down.

Neat trick: Look at the first note for bass clef, it looks like do in treble clef. In your mind, say do, then find the third – do re mi. The first note is mi, but an octave down from treble clef.

Exercise: Rewrite solfege exercise 11 in bass clef.

Sample 3

Write the number, then the note:

1. sol (whole note), 2. low si (quarter note), 3. hi re (half note), 4. fa (eighth note), 5. low la (dotted half note), 6. hi mi (dotted quarter note), 7. re (whole note), 8. la (quarter note), 9. hi do (half note), 10. hi sol (dotted quarter note)

If you finish, and this is correct, continue to **intermediate** level. Practice counting ledger lines. Write the number, and then figure out what each note is.

Advanced:

Look at the first page of Debussy's String Quartet. This is a very bad xerox copy and you can't even tell if something is sharp or natural!

Even worse, the third line says Alto and has a funny looking clef! The rule there is the line at the center of this clef is middle do. If that's true, then what normally looks like si is now middle do. For the third line, read the note, then think up one note. Si is do. Do is re.

1. What are your two flats?

2. Check the third line – do those two flats make sense here?

Now go through the marked areas and identify the almost invisible music marking, and explain why it *must* be what it is.

Notes for marked areas:

1. _____

2. _____

3. _____

4. _____
   _____

5. _____
   _____

6. _____

* * *

Sample 4

To begin learning to compose, we need to work step by step, starting with definitions. End goal: create a second harmonizing voice to a solfege exercise (candidates: 16, 17, 24, 25).

Intervals – unison, second, third, fourth, fifth, sixth, seventh, octave

1. **Consonance** – sound "agreeable". Unison, third, fifth, sixth, octave.

    "Perfect" consonance: unison, fifth, octave.

2. **Dissonant** - "lacking harmony". Second, fourth, seventh

Music motion – direct, contrary, oblique

- **Direct** – two voices go up or down in the same direction

    mi fa sol – give an example of a second voice going in direct motion, starting with do, then sol

- **Contrary** – one voice goes up while the other goes down

    si do re – give an example of a second voice going in contrary motion, starting with fa

- **Oblique** – one voice moves while the other stays the same

    sol la si do – experiment and find a note that sounds good when it stays the same

Basic rules ("training wheels" to start composing):

- *First rule:* From perfect consonance to perfect consonance, use contrary or oblique motion.

- *Second rule:* From perfect consonance to imperfect consonance, use any three motions.

- *Third rule:* From imperfect consonance to perfect consonance, use contrary or oblique.

- *Fourth rule:* From imperfect consonance to imperfect consonance, use any three motions.

Use the rules as guidelines to create a counterpoint both above and below the melody.

Archives

Several documents from the French School archives may also lend insight into the material presented in this guide. The first was written by the founders of French School, and the lecture was read at a recital on June 9th, 1928.

What is Solfeggio?

It is the science of music. Solfeggio is a science useful for all, for adults as well as for children, very pleasant to study when it is presented and taught according to a good method.

We do not ask pupils to do any homework. With one lesson each week, however, they will learn to read music at sight, to transpose at sight any melody whatsoever, to distinguish each tone of an instrument, of a voice or of an orchestra, immediately recognizing the notes, being able either to name them or to reproduce them on another instrument, or even to write them on paper ruled for music. All this is accomplished perfectly, the harmonies and time being an exact copy of what they have just heard.

We succeed in having any pupil accomplish this even if he shows no ability at all with special exercises for the training of the ear.

In our courses in Solfeggio we also teach our pupils, in addition to what we have just explained to you, style, musical interpretation, lives of composers and practical theory.

Of What Use is Solfeggio?

When one takes lessons in Solfeggio by this method, if the pupil is studying singing, the piano, the violin, the flute, the organ, or any other instrument whatsoever, he can read the most difficult musical passage without effort, as easily as if he were reading a book in his own language. In a word he actually enjoys musical complications! Why do children almost never like music or their music lessons? It is because of the great difficulty which they have in reading music. Why does one not read it as easily as his newspaper? And why should we not feel and understand music as easily as the printed statements which we read each day? You realize, we are sure, that the study of an instrument is easy if one has taken lessons in Solfeggio.

A pupil is capable, if you put any piece of music in his hands, simply by looking at it for the first time, to hear it with the ear of his imagination as well as if it were being rendered on a musical instrument - *he hears through his eyes!*

In a word, Solfeggio gives to pupils the right to call themselves musicians; even if they do not study any instrument, they acquire a musical culture sufficient to enable them to conduct an orchestra or a choir extemporaneously. If a pupil who has studied Solfeggio is one of an audience at a concert, he is at the same time one who enjoys the music, one who can evaluate it, and a critic of the first order. Is not the ability indicated by these names worth the trouble of studying Solfeggio?

These same pupils whom we have mentioned, while listening

to a concert, are able to select and isolate and write down any instrumental or orchestral theme which they have especially liked and which they wish to remember - just as one takes notes while listening to a lecture.

This method of teaching Solfeggio is that of the National Conservatory of Paris and is used here in Plainfield in our courses.

These same courses, which we give in Plainfield, were given with great success in Paris during eight years and then in several cities in Switzerland during twelve years. At Montreux alone we had one hundred pupils with whom we achieved surprising results.

We take children as young as four years and organize for that age a sort of "Kindergarten of Music" which admirably begins their music education.

The courses commence on the first of October, <u>although pupils may begin at any time in the year</u>; for in each course there are varied degrees of ability, and each time a part of the lesson is especially reserved for the beginners.

The courses in Solfeggio are taught in French or English according to the desire of the parents, and we repeat that they will necessitate no homework and that each pupil will be greatly interested since he will feel the charm of the method which we have described.

Yvonne Combe

(Graduate cum laude of the National Conservatory of Music, Paris)

Hélène Pfeiffer

(Pupil of Mlle. Combe, formerly teacher at the New School of Music, Montreux)

***

First part of an article in a 1950 New Jersey Music Magazine.

French School's Founders

Two musicians who reside and pursue their art in Plainfield, are Mlle. Yvonne Combe and Mlle. Helene Pfeiffer, founders of the French School of Music. Both have had colorful careers.

Yvonne Combe was born in Paris. Her grandmother (La Caiva) was a famous prima donna, who sang dramatic soprano leading roles for twenty-five years at the Paris Opera House before going on concert tours in all the great cities of France and other European countries. Yvonne's father died when she was a year old and she traveled with her grandmother for six or seven years, imbibing the tradition and atmosphere that surround a noted artist. She received her musical foundation through the teaching of her mother (the late Madame Louise H. Combe), a well-known vocal instructor. Madame Combe was an authoritative writer upon musical subjects. Her latest book, "Method of Vocal Education," was presented at the Beaux-Arts Institute of Paris and the manuscript of it was exhibited in the summer of 1937 at the International Exposition in Paris.

At the age of nine, Yvonne Combe entered the National Conservatory of Paris and continued her musical education there under the direction of Theodore Dubois (director of the Conservatoire) and Gabriel Faure. She advanced far in piano-virtuoso work with Marguerite Long, Paul Drop and Roger Ducasse.

Mlle. Combe gave me a signed copy of her mother's book: Méthode - Éducation Vocale - Louise H. Combe. At the end it says:

> LOUISE H. COMBE, Officier d'Académie
> École Nouvelle de Musique,
> Montreux (Suisse)

***

I will close these sections of background and historic material with one of several letters written to the "Tantes" at The French School of Music by Seymour Bernstein. The M.E.C. refers to the NJ Music Education Council, which held annual piano competitions. Two of his letters are typed (including this one), and the other is handwritten.

Nov. 17, 1964

My dear Tantes:

At last I have a chance to write to you.

I was at the M.E.C. concert last Sunday and was there, I must say, out of duty to the organization. But what I heard, especially from your pupils, was something so astonishing, so inspiring, that I feel it would have been a great loss to me had I not gone.

Perhaps Jim Correnti outplayed them all with his unusual sincerity and sensitivity and probably Robert Taub is a genius and will become a great pianist. And what are we to say of that incredible girl, Julie Jacobson? Amazing!

But now, what can we say to my dear Tantes who were responsible for such refined and mature playing. You must be truly great teachers. Your pupils testify to this fact and I am so proud to know you. You are the ones who should present the master lessons and set an example to all N.J. teachers. I can't recall ever hearing such musical values coupled with technical excellence from young N.J. pianists and my heart goes out to you in bravos and congratulations.

Sincerely,

Seymour Bernstein

Synesthesia

I was surprised to learn my brother-in-law has synesthesia, and since I was curious as to whether or not synesthesia could be used as a tool in developing or refining absolute pitch, I emailed him a series of questions. These were his responses:

> I think I can answer a few of these. First of all I don't think there's just one kind of color synesthesia. I did a bit of research into it when I first learned it was not an ordinary experience and I found some accounts that matched what I experience and many others that don't. Most of the academic treatments of it seem quick to associate the responses with changes in pitch. That's not what I experience. When it happens to me it's a function of changes in tone, timbre, sound texture, etc. Sometimes pitch change can trigger it but only if it also results in a change in the sound quality in some way. For example I dabble with synthesizers quite a bit and I've noticed that if I play say a pure sine wave and steadily lower the pitch through the octaves it will take on different characters due to the the inconsistent way the electronics(filters)+speakers(resonances)+room(reverbs) render the signal over the range. That can evoke some subtle synesthesia experiences for me, and I wonder if that effect is sometimes wrongly attributed to simply the pitch changing within studies that don't take all aspects into account.
>
> Also I don't think the colors are created by the brain. I think it's just a memory phenomenon where memories of sounds somehow get cross-referenced with memories of colors at a

very deep level. Like maybe when there's an unusual sound, the brain does a query to gather as much information about what it might be as possible, and for some reason color information is a response that overrides the others. The reason I think this is the case is because the colors I most often experience are the ones most common in the world around. Greens, blues, oranges, browns, violets and "metallic" colors like silver and gold. Noticeably missing are the purer shades of red. I've never experienced a red sound. Maybe if I wreck into a stop sign sometime that might change.

1. How do you manage the extra sensory information? Does this overwhelm people with synesthesia? How do you learn to deal with this?

In my case it's not an overwhelming experience. Just noticeable. I liken it to when you smell some kind of odor, good or bad, and it instantly reminds you of a situation, a place, a person, etc. It's not a conscious effort, it's just that somehow an experience has been associated with that particular odor in the memory banks, and it leaps out. That seems to be common with people and is probably a form of synesthesia itself. In the case of the color synesthesia sometimes when I hear certain sounds what I can only describe as color textures come instantly to mind. Like watercolor smudges. It's not an unpleasant thing and I don't really give it much thought although every once in awhile it does grab my attention in stronger ways (see below). I don't know why that is and I haven't found any consistent pattern to it.

2. Are you able to listen to music while you work, or is that distracting? Is it distracting if you drive and listen to music?

No it's not distracting in any way. When I listen to music I'm frequently thinking about other things anyway so it's just part of the noise.

3. Can you speak to what happens to people who have tinnitus?

No, but if I ever got tinnitus and it was "synesthesized" to a particular color that never changed then I could see how that might be frustrating.

4. What happens with people who have synesthesia who are color blind? And what is it like dealing with a greater level of information (ear) that maps to a lesser level of information (color blind eye).

That's an interesting question. I suspect they would recall whatever colors they are familiar with since they would be the colors that get cross-referenced in memory.

5. Do people who have synesthesia see the exact same things? For example, do is red, re is green, mi is blue, etc. Or do they differ? Someone else sees do is purple, re is pink, mi is teal.

That's another interesting one and I'll share a particular experience that makes me wonder. I was in a Barnes & Noble a few years ago and they were playing a song over the speakers that gave me a stronger than usual synesthesia episode. My thought was it was the orange-est song I'd ever heard. Like bursty multiple shades of orange. I was intrigued and I wrote down some of the lyrics and then looked it up when I got home (search on Youtube for "Junip Tide".) Advance to 3:50 where it starts a long sustained crescendo of piles of interesting textures.

Now notice the album cover. A sunset! Total coincidence? Maybe. Or maybe the cover artist experienced the same thing I did. By the way just about every song on the album sounds orange-ish to me. So there's something about the band's style, choice of instruments, arrangements, or something that they've knowingly or unknowingly reliably reproduced with respect to color synethesia.

The buzz sounds to me like a sawtooth wave from a synthesizer and that seemed to be the trigger in my mind. So I think the effect can be triggered on demand under the right circumstances and maybe these guys are being clever with that.

6. What about sharps and flats? And what is the unit of measure for color change? Is it whole steps, half steps, quarter steps? What happens when you hear a flat la flat? Are the changes gradual or discrete?

Again, for me it's not a function of pitch. Not directly. It's about tone and texture. Although I'd bet that by intentionally mixing a few pure waveforms together and then detuning some of them the result could evoke some syneth responses since it would create unique timbres. After all, that's the basis of additive synthesis. I'll try it sometime.

7. What happens when a car horn honks, someone clinks a glass, or a train rolls by?

All sudden very high frequency sounds are bluish-white to me. Cymbal crashes, breaking glass, whistles, etc. That's pretty much a constant. As are just about all sounds that stimulate ASMR (autonomous sensory meridian response). Very low frequency sounds have no color. Maybe they are unusual enough that I have no color memories to associate with them.

His summarized assessment:

I don't experience pure high saturation colors like in some of the reports. It's more like low saturation ambient lighting against smudgy backdrops with occasional flashes of brighter color. Like what you might see if you ran some slow motion video through an image processor that applied an extreme blur effect to it. The images would degrade to just one or a few dominant color smudges at any point in time. So my theory, for what it's worth, is that the effect is involuntary memory recall of imagery that's so poor that only a few colors bleed through. The defect is the involuntary recall that's stimulated by different sounds.

As for the correlation with pitch changes I don't understand that. Like Kanye West describes, the effect for me is consistent with the kind of sound maker involved. Piano has dominantly blue-ish tones no matter what note is played. Something about the timbre or harmonics or whatever of that instrument evokes that particular color experience. Collections of many rich sounds like in an orchestra can have a dominant color depending on what piece is being played. Different collective timbres at different moments I suppose.

Piano Practice

This section will augment both *Fundamentals of Piano Practice* and this solfege guide with relevant history and material related to piano practice, to show how solfege classes and piano lessons reinforce one another.

New Students

These instructions were given to me by Stephen Waters back in the late 1980s when I wanted to pick up a few piano students on the side, probably written by Mlle. Combe.

Piano Lessons for Young Beginners (How to Start)

1. <u>Learn</u> by heart: do re mi fa sol la si do / do si la sol fa mi re do (and C, D, E since that is the norm in the US...)

2. <u>Find</u> the notes on the keyboard

    a. in the order of the scale

    b. then jumping around

    c. focus the attention on the order of the black keys, two close together then three, alternating two and three. Every time there is a set of two black keys, find the do in front, then find all the dos, all the res, all the mis etc. (1 chip every three notes)

3. <u>Reward</u> every good answer or exact exercise with colored chips

4. <u>Position</u> of the fingers - very important - slightly curved, playing with tips.

    a. Little finger and thumb, being short, on the edge of the key The three longer fingers where they naturally fall.

b. No motion of the wrist, level with the arm, adjust seat accordingly with cushions or telephone books. Better yet, use an adjustable stool.

5. <u>Playing</u>

    a. Count slowly one-two for each finger to give time to concentrate on good position

    b. Do not hop or let go of the key until playing the next note

    c. Start on the high do next to the middle do for the right hand

    d. then the left hand on the next do down

    e. <u>Several times</u>, give a chip for each hand to reward the effort

6. <u>Le Carpentier</u>

    a. Page 10, #3 first, reading the notes, point to all the dos then all the res, then all the dos and the res, reward, then point to all the mis, then all the fas, then all the sols, then all the notes as they come in order, reward. (Name the notes as the teacher points to them)

    b. Play the notes and sing naming each note as you play, trying hard not to look at your fingers. Feel them keeping steady position, this becomes a must at the third lesson. (Do not mention position too much while the pupil concentrates on reading and playing these notes, one thing at a time.)

c. On the second week, if #3 is good, proceed the same way for #1 exercise, then #2 on third week and so on. Go to page 11 through treble clef exercises before starting bass clef exercises. Explain why middle do is above the staff with bass clef and below the staff with treble.

d. <u>Page 7</u> - Insist on counting out loud, focus attention on whole notes having 4 counts or beats, and quarter notes having only one each. Explain bar lines separating measures, each measure getting four counts whether there is one note or four notes to play. Then explain that each finger has a number and make the pupil show which one is #1, #4, #3, #2, #5 with each hand and refer to small black numbers above or below each note, or fingering, which they have to read mentally along with the notes while counting regularly aloud 1, 2, 3, 4 (indicated in first measure in red).

- First - right hand 5 times every day, second - left hand 5 times

- At the second lesson, try both hands together

- Go on from there only if the hand position is right, giving one line hands together and one line hands separate, every week

<u>Encourage</u> by praising any effort, and give chips as a reward. Have the pupil count them at the end of the lesson, giving stars. Keep star book dated and in order, just like a report card. Give prizes for solfege and piano.

Le Carpentier

This is now out of print, so the following pages with markings show how with an efficient number of exercises, new students could immediately begin building piano playing skills.

Piano students at French School worked on two things simultaneously:

1. Short exercises from Le Carpentier, Le Couppey, Czerny, etc. to slowly build skills, analogous to climbing up a ladder one rung at a time. The point wasn't necessarily to perfect the exercises, although many were musical enough they were performed at French School recitals.

2. Students would also be assigned a longer piece to learn (almost immediately).

This approach yields benefits over just playing pieces, or just focusing on exercises:

- Each exercise builds a new skill one rung at a time on the ladder. If students targeted the top of the ladder immediately without scaffolding their way to the top, this would be frustrating and counterproductive.

- Tackling a new short, self-contained exercise every couple weeks forces students to quickly evaluate and break down new music, reinforcing what is learned in solfege class.

- Tackling a larger piece builds skills related to endurance and discipline, and encourages students to learn effective strategies like working on the beginning and end of the piece first, and tackling the hardest parts first.

- After a number of exercises, when students have achieved a new level of competence, the number of pieces a student can play expands.

* * *

* * *

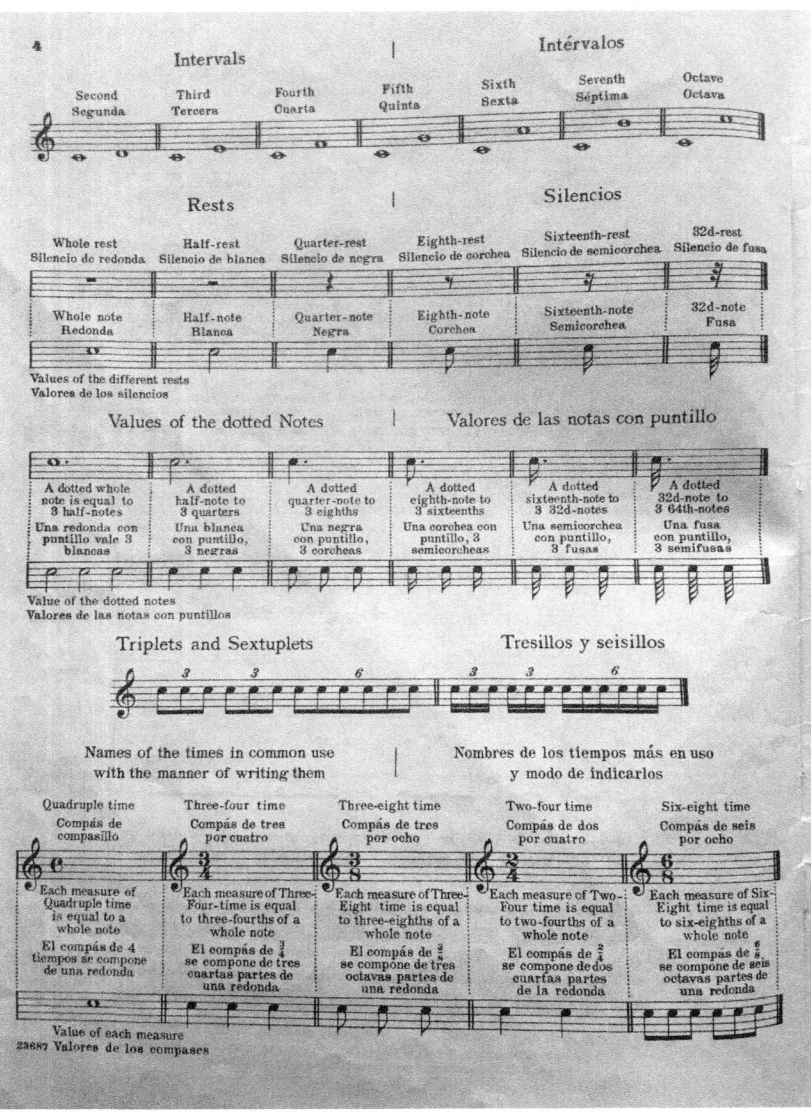

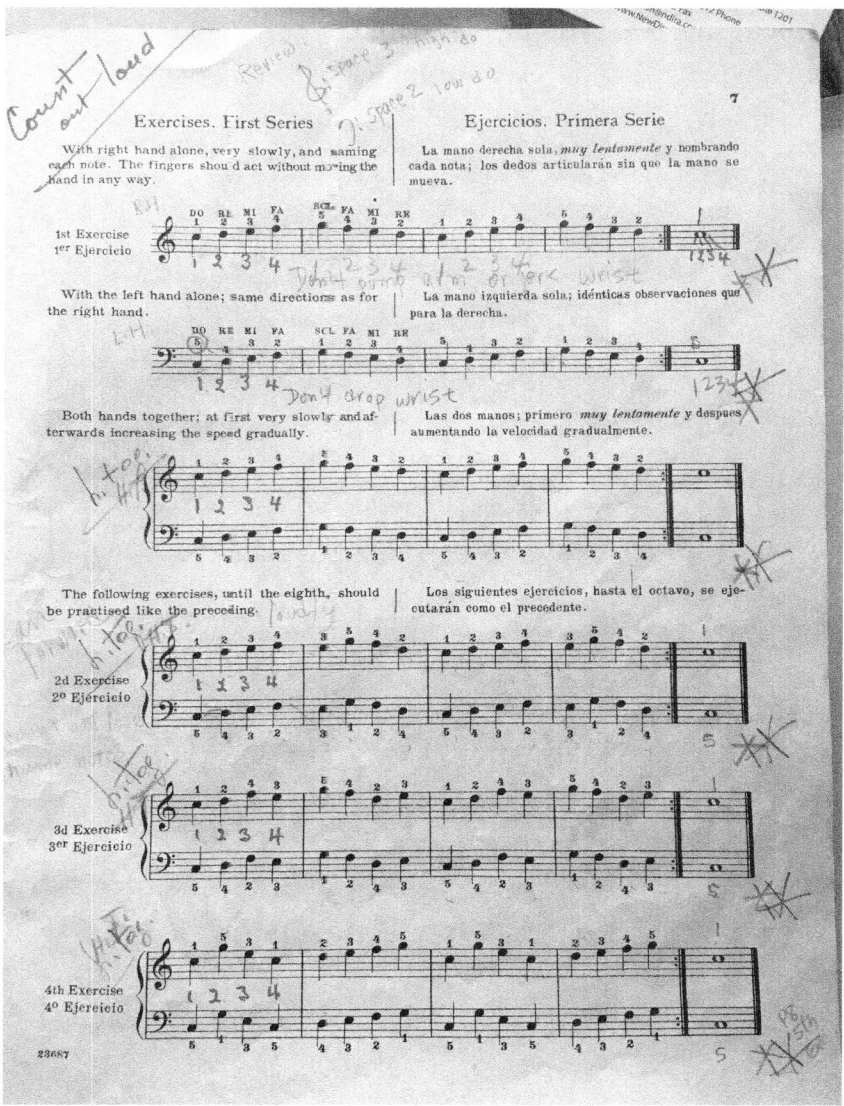

Students are assigned one or two lines each for a short exercise and a larger piece, to practice for the following week's lesson. Students would be assigned the new lines first H.S. for "hands separate", then H.Tog for "hands together". Students quickly learn the material by using the continuity rule, and rotate between practicing the exercise and piece so that they can periodically "get it and forget it".

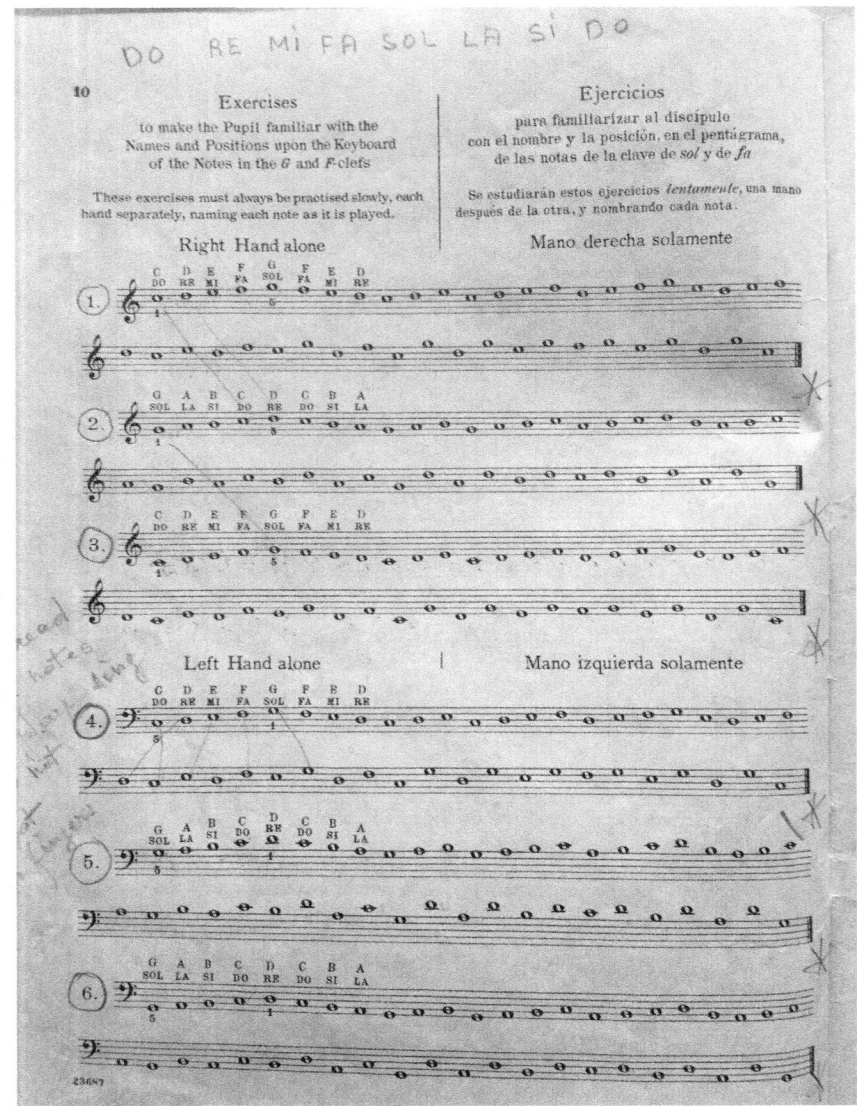

* * *

Some helpful handwritten comments in these pages:

- Count out loud
- Name notes
- Lean forward
- Don't pump arm or jerk wrist
- Don't drop wrist
- Play / sing
- Do not look at your fingers
- Don't rest non-playing fingers on keys
- Pretend play left hand (an excellent way to scaffold from hands separate to hands together)

Other comments worth adding:

- Don't seesaw
- Within a phrase, do not lift finger before the next note is played (learn to play legato)

Why is it so important that every piano student learn these fundamentals early on? Because regardless of age, skill, years of piano lessons, etc., these things scream amateur.

The key difference between French School alumni vs. many non-

French School alumni is that French School alumni, from day one, were taught how to become amateur professionals, as opposed to professional amateurs. There is a huge difference. What is important is whether a performer's overall behavior indicates they were taught how to be an amateur professional, because it is only amateur professionals who may someday become professional. The professional amateur has no hope of ever doing that, and those who understand what constitutes excellence know the difference between amateur professionals and professional amateurs.

* * *

As the exercises progress into short pieces, some may have B.H. at the end of the assigned portion, short for "by heart" or by memory. They may also have "fast", to indicate full speed.

Le Carpentier | 191

The entire process unfolds as follows for roughly two lines of music assigned each week depending on complexity:

- Hands separate, learn slow using the continuity rule

- Hands together slow, pretend playing left hand with continuity rule to scaffold to hands together.

- Memorize sooner rather than later, and check the music periodically to prevent practicing sightreading errors. Some teachers may disagree with this especially if a student isn't a particularly good at sightreading (which is understandable). To reiterate, use the hundreds of Dannhäuser solfege exercises for sightreading practice. Use instrument lesson time to refine technique and musicality, and practice memorization skills.

- As quickly as possible, begin thinking about the musicality first hands separate then together using the continuity rule. Why? By working on the musicality sooner, less needs to be unlearned. *Do not* learn the entire piece before working on the musicality. In fact, even if the notes are not fully mastered, start working on the musicality. If repetitive practice is needed anyway, the more it is practiced correctly from the start, the better. Also, memorizing the music first gives students the ability to concentrate fully on shaping the musicality.

- Add pedal, but continue to practice enough times without pedal as pedaling can hide technical problems.

- Hands separate to build up speed, using the continuity

rule

- Hands together at full speed

Tips and tricks for pedaling:

- Play-pedal - in other words, play the note first, then press the pedal

- Half pedal - half pedal means pressing the pedal just slightly to get a sustain. It is not necessary most of the time to press the pedal all the way down

- Flutter pedal - press pedal slightly and lift, press and lift. This is another way to get a sustain, without the pedal sounding muddy over time.

- When lifting the pedal, keep the foot in contact with the pedal. Do not raise the foot off the pedal and then slap the pedal on the way down

As to what references to use for today, since Le Carpentier is out of print, Alfred's has books for children and adults. They use alphabetic notation (CDE vs. do re mi).

References

Adler, Samuel. *The Study of Orchestration.* New York: W. W. Norton & Company, Third Edition, 2002,

Chang, Chuan C. *Fundamentals of Piano Practice.* Florida: Third Edition, 2016.

Dannhäuser, A. *Solfège des Solfèges.* New York: G. Shirmer, Inc., 1986.

Mann, Alfred. *The Study of Counterpoint - from Johann Joseph Fux's Gradus ad Parnassum.* New York: W. W. Norton & Company, 1965.

Miyazaki, Ken'ichi. *Learning Absolute Pitch by Children: A Cross-sectional Study.* Music Perception Volume 24, Issue 1. 2006.

Online References

William Wieland, music instructor: https://www3.northern.edu/wieland/index.htm

Online Courses

Make Music Now! Bootcamps, for Dannhaüser Solfège des Solfèges, Books I and II.

50 minute, free introductory webinar: Make Music Now! Webinar

Free downloads with the webinar:

- Why Solfege?

- Inside Scoop

https://eileensauer.podia.com

Acknowledgements

I want to express my deepest gratitude to Bob Marcus, who was my dad's boss when my dad was a physicist working at the AT&T Bell Laboratories think tank in Murray Hill, NJ. His daughters, Karen and Suzanne, took piano lessons at The French School of Music, and Bob's recommendation to my dad changed the course of our family's history. I can't begin to grasp how our lives would have unfolded without French School.

Mademoiselle Yvonne Combe, founder of French School, and her student, Stephen Waters, affected many lives over an almost 90 year period.

Judy Waters, this journey wouldn't have happened if you had not kept the school open. The French School of Music celebrated its 90th anniversary in October 2017 because of you, and the events that have unfolded since we restarted solfege classes helped us to understand how impactful the school was, and understand that what we learned from Mlle. Combe is worth passing along. Your family's sacrifice over many decades kept Yvonne Combe's legacy alive for new generations of music students.

My professors at Juilliard's Evening Division have added rich learning experiences over the years: Conrad Cummings, Dalit Warshaw, Evan Fein, Dan Ott, Ray Lustig, and Jude Vaclavik.

My conversations over the years with French School alumni Grace Boeringer, Louis Cyrille Martin, Carol Comune, Robert Taub, Vince Di Mura, Wendy Jaffe, Karen Zereconski, Suzanne and Tim Waters, Matthew Chow, Janet Borgobello, Yves Sukhu, and Arhant Rao have been extremely insightful.

Al Pendleton, my Chorale director at Governor Livingston Regional High School, started me on my journey as a composer through the Gifted and Talented Program during my senior year.

My solfege students made writing this solfege teaching guide possible. All of you have surprised me more than you will ever know.

I'm grateful to John Perez for his non-French School insights, as he is able to tell me exactly why a particular French School approach is so effective. Those of us who were lucky enough to be raised using French School methods can take what we had for granted, and be somewhat naive in our approach. It is because of John that I realized a vital component to teaching one generation to hand the torch to the next generation involves those trained in the French School method having immersive mentoring sessions with those not trained in the same way, to surface any blind spots. These blind spots need to be documented clearly, so that the French School method remain effective from generation to generation because people know how to adopt this method within the correct framework.

I'm grateful that our Chang family (dad Chuan, mom Merry, and sister Sue-Lynn) has enjoyed decades of interesting dinner conversations around music and French School. My brother-in-law David Hinson has had some interesting comments about synesthesia. And thank you to my husband Frank Sauer, for your support during one of life's most unexpected detours.

About the Author

A New Jersey-based composer of contemporary classical music and some jazz, Eileen's work spans piano, string, and wind instrumentations. She has studied composition, orchestration, and music production in The Juilliard School's Evening Division.

A former technologist (B.S. in Math - Computing from University of Notre Dame), she lives in Jersey City, NJ with her husband Frank and cat Cassie.

Printed in Great Britain
by Amazon